Caribbean Verse

also edited by O. R. DATHORNE

CARIBBEAN NARRATIVE

Caribbean Verse

an anthology

edited and introduced by

O. R. DATHORNE

HEINEMANN EDUCATIONAL BOOKS

LONDON

Heinemann Educational Books Ltd
22 Bedford Square, London WC1B 3HH
P.O. Box 1028, Kingston, Jamaica
27 Belmont Circular Road, Port of Spain, Trinidad
LONDON EDINBURGH MELBOURNE AUCKLAND
SINGAPORE HONG KONG KUALA LUMPUR
IBADAN NAIROBI NEW DELHI EXETER (NH)

ISBN 0 435 98220 6

© Heinemann Educational Books Ltd 1967
Introduction © O. R. Dathorne 1967
First published 1967
Reprinted 1971, 1974, 1979

Printed and bound in Great Britain by
Fakenham Press Limited, Fakenham, Norfolk

Contents

Acknowledgements

Thanks are due to the following for permission to include their poems in this volume: Raymond Barrow, Vera Bell, George Campbell, Martin Carter, Frank Collymore, John Figueroa, A. N. Forde, Wilson Harris, A. L. Hendriks, C. L. Herbert, E. McG. Keane, Walter MacA. Lawrence, Ian McDonald, Eric Roach, A. J. Seymour, Philip Sherlock, M. G. Smith, Harold Telemaque, Derek Walcott, and Daniel Williams. Thanks are also due to Basil McFarlane for permission to include poems by himself and his father, J. E. Clare McFarlane; to Mrs Jessie Dayes for poems by Roger Mais; and to Miss Ethel Marson for a poem by Una Marson.

Editor's Note

An invitation to Guyana made certain necessary contacts possible in the islands. I should like to express thanks to the staff of the BBC Library and the Institute of Jamaica, as well as to the entire library staff of the University of the West Indies and the University of Ibadan for co-operation and help. Also to several of the poets here who gave me factual information; and to Mrs Jessie Dayes, Miss Ethel Marson, Mrs Walcott, N. E. Cameron, and Cedric Lindo.

O. R. D.

for HILDE *and* SHADE CECILY

Flemni feros agitante suos sub sole iugales
Vivimus . . .

FRANCIS WILLIAMS
eighteenth-century Jamaican poet

Introduction

BECAUSE it is tempting to regard West Indian poets as novelists in the making it is necessary to attempt some just assessment of their achievements. At first sight there seems to be a great deal that is wrong with West Indian poetry—there are the ever-recurrent themes of seascape and landscape descriptions, a certain amount of religious hysteria and a melancholic pre-occupation with death. It is easy to dismiss this all as 'romantic', in the nineteenth-century sense, and to accuse West Indian poets of a blind adherence to an effete convention. But one must take into consideration the geographical setting within which the poets write, and certainly it cannot be denied that sea and natural scenery dominate the environment. The pertinent question, therefore, is what have these poets done with their environment? Have they utilized it imaginatively or merely indulged in an unhealthy relationship with it? Have they been simply content with spinning out ingenious metaphors to describe scenery or have they attempted more? The answer is partly to be found in an historical survey of the whole gamut of West Indian poetry.

When Derek Walcott said that 'West Indian literature originated in verse' he was only stating a half truth. What has happened is that the West Indian novel, which has extended its area of reference far beyond the West Indies, emanated from poets and therefore remained 'poetic' in form and language. But West Indian poets have remained closer both to their sources and to their initial medium. In a way this was to be expected for our society is one which, thankfully, is not geared to the wheels of industry and in a leisurely pastoral community, poetry is the language of belief in a familiar environment. The West Indian novelists were escaping, one suspects, not only to a more economically rewarding community, but to an environment where the images had already been charted for them by their very education in the West Indies. The poets who remained had few landmarks; the tradition they had inherited in poetry was a worthless one since both in metre and content it was itself related more to temperate latitudes. They had to re-organize a whole experience, to disentangle alien notions and codify their own domestic concepts.

It is no wonder that Roy Fuller in a B.B.C. broadcast in 1949 found a 'hotch-potch of styles' in the work of a West Indian poet. For the inheritance had been so varied. As early as the eighteenth century Francis Williams, a Jamaican and the son of freed slaves, wrote Latin panegyrics to successive governors in his island. He was born at the beginning of the century, the youngest of three sons, and educated in England at a grammar school and the University of Cambridge where he read Mathematics. He was a ward of the Duke of Montagu who wanted to discover, in the words of a contemporary:

> whether, by proper cultivation and a regular course of tuition at school and the university, a Negro might be found capable of literature as a white person.

Francis Williams lived until 1770 and proved his mettle so successfully that after returning to Jamaica and opening a school, he used to describe himself as 'a white man acting under a black skin'! Obviously therefore one will look in vain for anything faintly indigenous in what he wrote and,

2

for instance, in a long poem that survives in Latin he addressed Ovidian couplets to a current governor. However, he does show both some concern for his island and for his people, and there are references (albeit apologetic) to his colour. As he concludes this address:

> An island gave me birth, the famous Britons nurtured me—an island that will never be sad while you, her father, flourish. This is my prayer: may they see you ruling a vigorous people till the end of time. A land that is a dwelling-place of God.

The awe towards Britain and the claims to being West Indian were unspoken issues that were to continue to dominate our writing until the twentieth century. There is no continuous tradition from Francis Williams, but he adequately expresses the predicament of the West Indian poet, trapped between a futile adoration for Empire and a muffled love for home. God is the unifying factor.

Equally no direct link can be said to exist between modern West Indian poets and folk-songs, although it is certain that some of these rhythms continue to dominate contemporary West Indian poetry. The dialect verse of Claude McKay and Louise Bennett could not have been written without this folk-tradition which is to do with a new way of *seeing* as well as of *hearing*. It is this concept that nurtures the roots of West Indian poetry—Sherlock's Daley and Macdonald's Jaffo are sad and comical figures whose pedigree derives from their closeness to the soil. When Lamming said that the work of West Indian writers was 'shot through and through with the urgency of peasant life' he was really describing the closeness of West Indian writing to a folk-tradition. It is possible of course that because calypsoes have monopolized some of the qualities of folk-songs (the chorus, communal concern, humour, complaint and so on), that these concerns have therefore been denied the written

3

composer of verse, who has tended to take his models from written European forms.

For closest to the West Indian poet were the models of Europeans who had written about the West Indies and who had adopted exotic attitudes to tropical landscape. Equally unrealistic was their view of the communities in which they found themselves: M. J. Chapman spoke of the 'song and jocund laugh' of the slaves who he felt were happy in their drudgery, but Simon Christian Oliver, a Guyanese Negro schoolmaster, who wrote in 1838, told another side to the drama of human degradation and suffering:

> Oh! ye first of August freed men who now liberty enjoy;
> Salute the day and shout hurrah to Queen Victoria;
> On this glad day the galling chains of Slavery were broke
> From off the neck of Afric's sons who bled beneath its yoke.

This not good poetry but it illustrates still another aspect to the bewilderment that was observed in Francis Williams; both poets acknoweldge their origins but address the over-lord with gratitude. It was another two centuries before Vera Bell and Martin Carter could adopt a different attitude to slavery and the real meaning of their historical association with Europe.

Egbert Martin, who wrote under the pen-name of Leo, was possibly the true ancestor of West Indian verse. His first book of poems was published in 1883 but his poetry suffers from certain defects—what Ian McDonald has called his 'sentimental and sickly-sweet phraseology'. One can also add to this the monotony of a great deal of his subject-matter, what he himself listed in his poem 'Themes of Song' as 'splendour', 'beauty' and 'music'. Poems like 'The Swallow' and 'Twilight' are typical of his verse with their flaccid nature descriptions, while his love-poems lack any true feeling. But although it is unlikely that either Tom Redcam or Constance

4

Hollar could have known anything about him, he, like they, helped to pioneer the writing of West Indian verse.

No one can doubt Tom Redcam's genuine love for Jamaica and for the Jamaican landscape, but it was a stranger's love; his great-grandfather had emigrated from Ireland in the eighteenth century and illness forced Redcam himself to go to England in 1921 where he died. It was as a stranger that he nostalgically remembered Jamaica:

> For England is England who mothers my soul,
> Truth, bare in its glory, with her deep self-control . . .
> But my little green island, far over the sea,
> At eve-tide, Jamaica, my heart is with thee.

It was an expatriate's Jamaica—of lush palm trees at evening and blue seas; indeed one feels that many of his poems could have been written by anyone. Tom Redcam (1870–1933) whose real name was Thomas MacDermot, was honoured as Jamaica's first poet laureate and was described by Walter Adolphe Roberts as a writer who gave to Jamaica 'a literature distinct from other lands'. But this was very likely written out of gratitude for Redcam's contribution in helping to foster Jamaican culture. Apart from his pieces of obvious dedication, there are poems on love, death, friendship, parting and religion which owe absolutely nothing to the fact that he was born in Jamaica. In verses like these, when he is not soothing us with flattering landscape descriptions, we see him at his worst. In 'To the Only Wise God' he is capable of writing doggerel like this:

> Therefore, I will appear
> Before Him without fear,
> And stand before Him there . . .

Or, in another poem about friendship, trite sentiments of this nature:

> Remember friend of mine
>> We're friends forevermore
> For that be braver, be thou strong,
>> And faithful more and more.

Redcam was no poet and Basil McFarlane was right when he suggested that Redcam's 'enthusiasm remains the most captivating feature' of his poetry. This praise is not as negligible as it seems when it is realized that it was his enthusiasm which encouraged a great many other poets to write.

Later writers were to take up social issues, but the first generation of West Indian poets saw landscape with an alien eye. The Jamaican, Constance Hollar (1880–1945), is a poet like this, and in her 'Poem' about how she captures and then sets free an insect, there is not only rather old-fashioned versifying but also an over-refined kind of vocabulary:

> A handful of beating softness,
> Two eyes that sparkle and glow,
> Wings that are covered with gold dust,
> You trample and flutter so.
> You will beat your downy pinions,
> You will lie all broken and dead,
> If you heed the lure and sparkle
> Of the bright lights overhead.

There is nothing 'West Indian' either in the observations or in the language, and if it is difficult to say what is meant by 'West Indian', at least we can be negatively certain about what is not. Often Constance Hollar used references to the classics ('Apollo's golden chariot', 'Aurora's far flung bars') to describe with jarring artificiality the world round her. When Una Marson spoke of how 'her poetry radiates all the joy she felt in simple things' she was certainly not referring to Constance Hollar's style, heavily encumbered with classical allusion.

West Indian poetry was developing in a certain direction —the overt description of nature, always from the point of view of an outsider, and nearly always in the manner of English nineteenth-century romanticism. To a large extent this is what several of our less successful modern poets have inherited. But Walter Adolphe Roberts in his *Pierrot Wounded and Other Poems* (1919) transferred a great deal of the affected love for the West Indies to France, and did far more for West Indian poetry than any of his forerunners. For when he wrote:

> I, the France of the brave, bright torch
> > I have been raped and have drunk of gall.
> Ruthless, the alien cannons scorch
> > Forest and orchard, hovel, hall . . .

he was expressing sentiments that Claude McKay could share at a later date, and he was employing a medium through which we can still respond. When thirty-one years later he published 'Villanelle of Jamaica', the topic had changed but the vocabulary remained that of a poet, not a versifier:

> Forever the white sea-horses charge the strand
> > Charge the powdered coral, the palms that lean
> But deep in the island my valley is warm and bland.
>
> Flowers are ardent here as a burning brand
> > Scarlet hibiscus and orchids of royal sheen
> Forever the white sea-horses charge the strand.

They are lines which the younger Walcott might well have written and they establish the claim that Adolphe Roberts has on our attention.

Until the 1920's there is no tough underlayer of social feeling in West Indian verse. The poet is the romanticized figure of Alfred Mendes's *The Poet's Quest* (1927) who goes

wandering through monotonous couplets of iambic penta-
meters in search of nature and love. Claude McKay's poetry,
of which the first two volumes appeared in 1912, introduced
a social note, and utilized what Walcott has called in another
context 'the raw spontanaeity of dialect'. Only these dialect
poems in the volume seem to work; those simply written
about friends or landscape do not succeed. There is no real
love of people and place in McKay, only in so far as they can
express ideas, his ideas. And so his vendor only functions
because she is identified with the down-trodden:

> Ef me no wuk, me boun' fe tief;
> S'pose dat will please the police chief;
> De prison dem mus' be wan' full
> Mak dem's 'pon we like ravin' bull.

In reality she is the poet's mouthpiece.

In another volume, in 'Whe' fe do?', the poet himself
questions the whole meaning of existence:

> We'll try an' live as any man,
> An' fight de wul' de best we can,
> E'en though it hard fe understan'
>   Whe' we mus' do.

These dialect poems are his earliest and his best; they are
closest to folk-tradition and are truly West Indian in language
and feeling. The sentiments of Marcus Garvey might have
been the same* but Garvey had neither the language nor the
idiom to express himself. In Garvey the message was upper-

---

* McKay wrote in *A Long Way from Home* (1937) about Garvey:
  A West Indian charlatan came to this country, full of antiquated
  social ideas; yet within a decade he aroused the social consciousness of
  the Negro masses more than any leader ever did, p. 354.
He did not believe in Garvey but he sympathized with his beliefs and ideals.
Where the two men differed is that Garvey saw the return to Africa in real
physical terms, McKay as a matter of mental re-adjustment.

8

most, his strong pro-black, anti-white feelings taking the place of any serious attempt to write verse. Frequently what he wrote bordered closely on nonsense:

> Africa's millions laughed with the sun,
> In the cycle of man a course to run;
> In stepped the white man, bloody and grim,
> The light of these people's freedom to dim.

If, as Arthur Drayton has said in an article, the theme of Africa entered the path of West Indian poetry with McKay's verse, then with Garvey's it certainly found itself in a blind alley.

By the 1930's two anthologies had appeared—a Jamaican one in 1929 and a Guyanese in 1931. There is no denying the fact that it was praise-worthy that little under a hundred years after the abolition of slavery such a volume of poetry could exist. But many of the poets in these anthologies were imaginatively expatriates, and if they wrote about our islands and our sea, they could not view them with our eyes. But a beginning had been made and the work of J. E. Clare McFarlane and Una Marson in the thirties, George Campbell and A. J. Seymour in the forties prepared the way for a whole new generation of poets. In the forties too, the magazines *Bim* (Barbados), *Focus* (Jamaica) and *Kyk-over-al* (Guyana) all had their first issues and Henry Swanzy began editing 'Caribbean Voices' for the B.B.C. With these efforts West Indian verse was well and truly launched.

Our poets of the 1930's took only a little from McKay and Garvey but a great deal from the nature poetry of the previous generation. Like Vivian Virtue their observation was often from the natural world:

> Parting my window to the light
> That flooded up at April dawn
> Mine was a vision rare and bright . . .

9

They were not able to tell us why. They assumed that their readers (and it must be emphasized that they were writing for West Indians), must like sea and sunlight. But they made a conscious effort to make their poetry local; theirs was not the observation of writers imaginatively removed from the world they were describing, and even if, like Una Marson in 'Darlingford', they were at times unpoetical, they were at least always local and topical. The beginning of the application of landscape was made by Roger Mais in his very famous poem, 'All Men Come to the Hills', where nature began to signify a new potent duality, not unconnected with the growth of West Indian nationalism in the thirties. When Mais wrote of:

> men with dusty, broken feet;
> Proud men, lone men like me,
> Seeking again the soul's deeps—
> Of a shallow grave
> Far from the tumult of the wave—

he was describing the plight and the hope of the very workers that the Guyanese Martin Carter was to write about in his 'University of Hunger' almost two decades later. It was an inheritance from McKay, the utilization of poetry for expressing social discontent, but it was wedded to the glorification of nature. There was an intentional rejection of the platitudes that have been observed in some of the earlier poets; as H. P. Carberry was to write:

> We have neither Summer nor Winter
> Neither Autumn nor Spring
>
> We have instead the days
> When gold sun shines in the lush cane fields—
> Magnificently.

Whether like J. E. Clare McFarlane, Arthur Seymour and

Frank Collymore, they emphasized the natural world, or like George Campbell, Vera Bell and Philip Sherlock, the social environment, in none of them was landscape any longer the passive object of the poet's ecstasies. It had become an instrument for change. J. E. Clare McFarlane makes the heroine of *Daphne* (1931) say:

> Here are the musings of our country's poets,
> The aspirations of their song, the fruit
> And offspring of the labouring souls that strive
> For truth and beauty, born of love and shap'd
> To music; all the grace for which we yearn
> The pure white soul of Kingston from her mire
> Cleans'd and uplifted—that which now she is
> By the sure prophesyings of our hearts ...

To those poets of the thirties and forties, the peculiar vision of the poet was not an escape from life, as Mendes saw it, but an entrance, a face to face collision with disaster. George Campbell went further than any of the others: the poet was

> Not image of God
> Not image of man.
>
> So near to God
> So far from man.

He attempted to free the writer from all strictures.

Freeing the poet meant liberating both his subject-matter and his medium of expression. Until the late forties, with little exception, West Indian poetry had remained geared to strict metre and rigid rhyme-scheme. But George Campbell had championed freedom of subject-matter and style and incidentally insisted on a greater kind of responsibility. It was this that the younger McFarlane had inherited, although he was interested in the experience of religion through poetry. Derek Walcott, who was concerned with the manifestation of varied experiences on his own personality, and Wilson Harris who, in one of his periods, attempted a re-living of classical legends and a translation of them into the terms of his own time.

In the fifties and sixties West Indian poets are therefore no longer content with flat passive attitudes towards the natural world. A technological explosion has taken place in their sensibility, the result of which is that there is a renewed *application* of nature. Eric Roach, although of an older generation, belongs in mood and feeling to this period, but the dominant figure of the group is undoubtedly Derek Walcott, who had published his first book of verse in 1948. What these poets are doing is rejecting the assumptions which two generations of nature poets had made about their world; instead there is a complete imaginative re-ordering.

There has been a renewed interest in dialect, distrusted so long as 'bad English'. When Knolly S La Fortune writes in 'Carnival Rhapsody':

> Beat dem drums
> Boys beat dem drums
> Fast and loud and sweet,
> Dey go ge we consolation
> Dey go ease we sufferation . . .

we recognize that he is employing our English as no non-West Indian could. McKay had done it in the manner of a complaint, La Fortune is using all its vigour to describe a dance. Similarly Louise Bennett has never received sufficient praise for her own inventiveness. She has maintained a balance; 'the comic mask', which Salkey assures us, West Indian writers wear 'with more assurance than the tragic', is seldom donned by poets. But Louise Bennett does this and succeeds: the object of her satire in 'Pon Film' can be easily recognized:

> Dear Cousin Jim, eena film,
> Me ackin like a war!
> Dem call me 'movies extra', but
> Me call meself 'film-star.'

Equally one can see the solemnity beneath her comment on Jamaican independence:

> Independence wid a vengeance!
> Independence raisin Cain!
> Jamaica start grow beard, ah hope
> We chin can stand de strain!

Social protest in a modified use of dialect, is best seen in Sherlock's tragic poem about the plumber. For all of these poets are voicing the agonies of the inarticulate, those with whom Basil McFarlane identifies himself when he writes, almost in paranthesis:

> And God!
> I have no voice.

These are the same people to whom Walcott refers time and time again in his verse—the peasants, the farmers, ourselves.

In Walcott's earliest volume of verse, published when he was just eighteen, he had written about his people who were continuously exposed to the prying eyes of tourists whom he bitterly called 'the brassy visitors from hard cities in coloured shirts'. But initially Walcott's poetry was to do with the profound experience of growth into manhood. His boyhood view of childhood was, to say the least, startling:

> childhood is
> A vacant waiting for the contagion.

What redeemed the poetry of these early years was a strong religious sense which prevented it from being too anatomically morbid. The poem 'In a Year', written by a boy then still in his teens, reads like the words of a prematurely aged seer:

> Come, look a child
> Said the strong world in leaves
> Do you hear the waves walk, the clouds toss
> For your green love?

As John Figueroa has rightly added—two of the dominant themes in this early poetry were the loss of faith and the loss of love. But the fire symbol is both destroyer and preserver. As Walcott said in Canto IX of Walcott's *Epitaph for the Young*:

> O my son, the fire,
> That burns, refines, remember the city,
> Remember me.
> Although violence undoes us, by violence we are cleaned.

And just as the Castries fire came to stand for something larger in the poet's own life and the life of the islanders, so his own biography becomes identical with the history of his island. His development from boyhood, to the 'profound cigarette', and to the 'knife turning in the bowels' was an alteration from the spiritual, to the material and the sensuous on a personal level, and in terms of his island, a process of change from the slumber of colonial days to an awakening into new national feeling. The 'reluctant leopard of the slow eyes' was the truth that all had to face—the boy that grows into man, and the colonials that become a nation. A late poem 'Laventville' confirms the truth, bitter as it is, about the slave past 'whose horrors we all shared'.

Peter Abrahams wrote in his introduction to the *Independence Anthology of Jamaican Literature* that:

If the writer elects not to be concerned with the human and social problem of his own emerging society, that is his business. There may be those of us who think that since all good art must be bedded in the realities of life any escapist or tourist guide type of fiction which trades on the exotic setting or quaintness of speech will not be great or even very good. But we cannot impose this view on the writer.

This might almost be a comment on the development of the poetry which has just been examined. For whatever opinion we may hold about the function of art, this much is evident, that West Indian poets were most successful when they managed to free themselves from their incestuous relationship with landscape. And it was not only landscape from which George Campbell sought to release them, but from the reliance on foreign conventions which became a substitute for real feeling. In their introduction to *Burnt Bush*, H. M. Telemaque and A. M. Clarke spoke of how their imagery was drawn 'from the pulsing experiences we could abstract from these lovely islands . . . and not from a literary tradition', and theirs was a plea for a return to primary sources.

If I have charted the course of West Indian poetry as if there were no confluences, I do not mean to imply that the literature had neither source nor outlet, but that its origins were domestic. And the literary influences of the Bible, Eliot, Yeats, Wordsworth, like the language influences, are only what *we* have chosen to make of these. In other words both English Literature and Language have been forced into a West Indianizing process. Our novelists have been lured into immigration and necessary alienation, but our poets have remained as attendants and surgeons of our word. In the past they reminded us of the necessity for a novel dialogue and vision, in the future they will open up for us capacities into which we must enter if we are to preserve our own truths.

Raymond Barrow/*Dawn is a Fisherman*

Dawn is a fisherman, his harpoon of light
Poised for a throw—so swiftly morning comes:
The darkness squats upon the sleeping land
Like a flung cast-net, and the black shapes of boats
Lie hunched like nesting turtles
On the flat calm of the sea.

Among the trees the houses peep at the stars
Blinking farewell; and half-awakened birds
Hurtle across the vista, some in the distance
Giving their voice self-criticized auditions.   10

Warning comes from the cocks, their necks distended
Like city trumpeters: and suddenly
Between the straggling fences of grey cloud
The sun, a barefoot boy, strides briskly up
The curved beach of the sky, flinging his greetings
Warmly in all directions, laughingly saying
Up, up, the day is here! Another day is here!

Raymond Barrow/*There is a mystic splendour*

There is a mystic splendour that one feels
Walking this shore in the half-light of dawn,
Placing one's footprints on the sands where keels
Of ancient vessels must have beached and drawn.

For there are tales that speak of glorious days
When martial shouting rang within our Bay,
And cannons thundered, and black battle haze
Clouded this sickle isle with dark affray.

Those were the times when privateers fled
The predatory Brethren of the Coast;   10
Pirates and buccaneers—all these are dead,
And all their lordly sway seems but a ghost.

But even now the surf's loud thunder brings
Sound strangely clear—like battle cries of old;
And palm trees murmur of deep-sunken things,
Of buried treasure chests . . . and Morgan's gold . . .

Vera Bell/*Ancestor on the auction block*

Ancestor on the auction block
Across the years your eyes seek mine
Compelling me to look.
I see your shackled feet
Your primitive black face
I see your humiliation
And turn away
Ashamed.

17

Across the years your eyes seek mine
Compelling me to look   10
Is this mean creature that I see
Myself?
Ashamed to look
Because of myself ashamed
Shackled by my own ignorance
I stand
A slave.

Humiliated
I cry to the eternal abyss
For understanding   20
Ancestor on the auction block
Across the years your eyes meet mine
Electric
I am transformed
My freedom is within myself.

I look you in the eyes and see
The spirit of God eternal
Of this only need I be ashamed
Of blindness to the God within me
The same God who dwelt within you   30
The same eternal God
Who shall dwell
In generations yet unborn.

Ancestor on the auction block
Across the years
I look

I see you sweating, toiling, suffering
Within your loins I see the seed
Of multitudes
From your labour   40
Grow roads, aqueducts, cultivation
A new country is born
Yours was the task to clear the ground
Mine be the task to build.

George Campbell/*History makers*

I

Women stone breakers
Hammers and rocks
Tired child makers
Haphazard frocks.
Strong thigh
Rigid head
Bent nigh
Hard white piles
Of stone
Under hot sky   10
In the gully bed.

II

No smiles
No sigh
No moan.

III

Women child bearers
Pregnant frocks
Wilful toil sharers
Destiny shapers
History makers
Hammers and rocks.   20

George Campbell/*Litany*

I hold the splendid daylight in my hands
Inwardly grateful for a lovely day.
Thank you life.
Daylight like a fine fan spread from my hands
Daylight like scarlet poinsettia
Daylight like yellow cassia flowers
Daylight like clean water
Daylight like green cacti
Daylight like sea sparkling with white horses
Daylight like tropic hills   10
Daylight like a sacrament in my hands.
Amen.

George Campbell/*Oh! you build a house*

Oh! you build a house as a woman
Builds a child in her time, building
With the inner vision of her eyes
The knowingness of her being
The whole of her living, turned inward, creating.

Here you build a cottage in the hills
And raise up trees every leaf of them
As parents build up their children, wilfully.

Who would construct the sky?
Do you know how many visions   10
Of space to fill the view of your vision?
Where are the unseeing hands that would
Lift up one transfiguration of space
That a child would dream?

Yet you build like the builder of space
The weaver of silences, the construction of hills
With hands of existence, your purpose, the light of your way.
I would not tell you that, were it not natural,
Else I would turn away, mad like a man
From a mirror who sees the sky in his face   20
And the resolutions of horror and peace in his face.

Here you build your peace in ycur hills
Reconstructing your silences, like a child
Being endlessly born in its mother.

Here you construct your space, every forgetfulness,
Every pocket of silence, every atom of thought.
Here is the reconstruction of peace, never outside one,
But where a man can turn his energies
To his innermost being, to his own infiniteness.

Where are the succession of stars that are   30
The glory to one's mind,
Where is the space and the time that can be
The peace that man should know?
Yes! It's good that you build your cottage
And the external comforts of home.
'Tis the same process and reality backward.

The man in his own inner mind, on his own inner road,
On the most communal journey in the world,
The journey through one to the world of men,
Here, creatively, in the depths of silence   40
Amidst atomic laughter, the forestry of death,
Elusive simplicity of peace
Must a man build finally . . .

The reconstruction that is rebirth in motherhood,
The working of a plot of land,
The building of a house in the dirt,
The growing of grass, warm roses and trees
Reconstruction of the hills, mass upon mass
Resurrection of the sky, space beyond space:
The infinity of peace.   50

Martin Carter/*University of hunger*

Is the university of hunger the wide waste
is the pilgrimage of man the long march.
The print of hunger wanders in the land
the green tree bends above the long forgotten
the plains of life rise up and fall in spasms
the huts of men are fused in misery.

They come treading in the hoofmarks of the mule
passing the ancient bridge
the grave of pride
the sudden flight   10
the terror and the time.

They come from the distant village of the flood
passing from middle air to middle earth
in the common hours of nakedness.
Twin bars of hunger mark their metal brow
twin seasons mock them
parching drought and flood

is the dark ones
the half sunken in the land
is they who had no voice in the emptiness   20
in the unbelievable
in the shadowless.

They come treading on the mud floor of the year
mingling with dark heavy waters
and the sea sound of the eyeless flitting bat.

O long is the march of man and long is the life
and wide is the span.

is air dust and the long distance of memory
is the hour of rain when sleepless toads are silent
is broken chimneys smokeless in the wind   30
is brown trash huts and jagged mounds of iron.

They come in long lines
toward the broad city.
Is the golden moon like a big coin in the sky
is the flood of bone beneath the floor of flesh
is the beak of sickness breaking on the stone.
O long is the march of men and long is the life
and wide is the span.
O cold is the cruel wind blowing
O cold is the hoe in the ground.   40

They come like sea birds
flapping in the wake of a boat
is the torture of sunset in purple bandages
is the powder of fire spread like dust in the twilight
is the water melodies of white foam on wrinkled sand.

The long streets of night move up and down
baring the thighs of a woman
and the cavern of generation
The beating drum returns and dies away
the bearded men fall down and go to sleep   50
the cocks of dawn stand up and crow like bugles.

is they who rose early in the morning
watching the moon die in the dawn
is they who heard the shell blow and the iron clang
is they who had no voice in the emptiness
in the unbelievable
in the shadowless
O long is the march of men and long is the life
and wide is the span.

Frank Collymore/*Beneath the casuarinas*

We walk slowly beneath the casuarinas,
    Our feet make no sound on the thick pile spread
Beneath the trees' shade: all is silent:
    We walk with muted footsteps and no word is said.
Overhead the casuarinas strain upward to the sky,
    Their dull green plumage vainly poised for flight;
Around us everything is strange and still
    And all is filled with an unreal light;
We might be walking along the timeless floor
    Of a sea where desolate tides forever creep,   10
Or roaming along the secret paths
    That wind among the twilight plains of sleep.
And then . . . what is that sound which falls
    On the ear in the stillness? Is it the beat
Of the blood in the pulse, or the sigh
    Of the casuarinas in the midday heat?

The sound of the sea in the curled shell pressed
   To the eager ear . . . hearts' lost content . . .
The empty mouthing of the long-forgotten dead . . .
   The winds' secret . . . the old lament   20
Of all creation . . . silence made manifest
   In sound? We shall never know.
We pass from their shadow out into the sunlight,
   And the silence echoes and re-echoes within us as we go.

Frank Collymore/*Hymn to the sea*

Like all who live on small islands
I must always be remembering the sea,
Being always cognizant of her presence; viewing
Her through apertures in the foliage; hearing,
When the wind is from the south, her music, and smelling
The warm rankness of her; tasting
And feeling her kisses on bright sunbathed days;
I must always be remembering the sea.

Always, always the encircling sea,
Eternal: lazylapping, crisscrossed with stillness;   10
Or windruffed, aglitter with gold; and the surf
Waist-high for children, or horses for Titans;
Her lullaby, her singing, her moaning; on sands,
On shingle, on breakwater, and on rock;
By sunlight, starlight, moonlight, darkness:
I must always be remembering the sea.

Go down to the sea upon this random day
By metalled road, by sandway, by rockpath,
And come to her. Upon the polished jetsam,
Shell and stone and weed and saltfruit   20
Torn from the underwater continents, cast
Your garments and despondencies; re-enter
Her embracing womb: a return, a completion.
I must always be remembering the sea.

Life came from the sea, and once a goddess arose
Fullgrown from the saltdeep; love
Flows from the sea, a flood; and the food
Of islanders is reaped from the sea's harvest,
And not only life and sustenance; visions, too,
Are born of the sea; the patterning of her rhythm   30
Finds echoes within the musing mind.
I must always be remembering the sea.

Symbol of fruitfulness, symbol of barrenness,
Mother and destroyer, the calm and the storm!
Life and desire and dreams and death
Are born of the sea; this swarming land
Her creation, her signature set upon the salt ooze
To blossom into life; and the red hibiscus
And the red roofs burn more brightly against her blue.
I must always be remembering the sea.   40

Frank Collymore/*Return*

We too shall come down to the sea,
Past the gay green gardens of the heart's munificence,
Past the lichened pathway where the rust
Stains the stone and the forked tree stands desolate,
Down to the sands
Where the shattered bones of leviathan
Are strewn with coral splinters and the wrack of lands.

We shall come down to the sea again
Whence we once crawled landward
To rear our gardens and palaces and temples;   10
For always there has lingered, echoing the ancient memory
Within the bone,
Persistent, the song of the sea-shell:
And naught shall silence that insistent monotone.

We shall return. See,
On the bright sands her waves have strewn
Golden coronals to welcome us!
Crowned as kings we shall return—
We who have fled
From her dark embrace, back to our mother, the sea,   20
The crowding sea, vomiting her living and her dead.

John Figueroa/*Birth is . . .*

Birth is too bloody; we resist the end
The throes, the after-birth and after-care
Of child and mother. Darkly unaware
We start the perfumed path whose sudden bend
At dawn to us reveals the unknown friend.
The agony of mother and child we fear,
We are solicitious, nor God nor air
We trust without security we will not lend

Our precious selves to poor posterity.
Suppose our seed to Faith should swell   10
And make demands on our temerity!
Or throes like waves should dash the spell
That dreams ourselves the final verity
Against infinite shores to splintered shell.

John Figueroa/*Oedipus at Colonus*

I come to these mountains
I Oedipus though blind
Can see the tops gently
Touched with white the dawn blue
As clean as my purged self
I come at dawn to wait for dusk.

When the life-giver has warmed
Away the silver lace of dew
And warmed this sacred grove
After noon he will withdraw   10
Beneath the crisp whiteness
Of the round mountain in the west there.
The cooling grove shall darken
And grow secret
I shall follow him into the dusk
Below the peak.

Daughters, when the sun and thy father
Leave thee in saffron shadows
Consider my life's day-tramp here,
Seek not yet to know what night brings.   20

A. N. Forde/*Canes by the roadside*

Time was
you tossed in a delirium
of whispers near the roadside:
now your last whisper
is a treasury of lost sound

Months ago
you were a handful
of green ribbons teasing the wind:
now dead strips tell
where the colour and the sparkle go.   10

In the cycle

of things you will submit
to the tyranny of shining teeth
and the remorseless murmur of the mill
and all your once-green pride will not console a bit.

Heaped up
in your pyre ready for
the yearly sacrifices to power
you lie robbed of the majesty
of your plotted earth   20
bared of the eagerness of your dream.

Wilson Harris/*Troy*

The working muses nourish Hector
hero of time: like small roots that move
greener leaves to fathom the earth.
This is the controversial tree of time
beneath whose warring branches
the sparks of history fall. So eternity to season, it is converted
    into
an exotic roof for love, the barbaric conflict of man.

So he must die first to be free.
Solid or uprooted in pain, his bright limbs
must yield their glorious intentions to the secret   10

root of the heart. And musing waters dart
like arrows of memory over him, a visionary: smarting tears
of the salty earth.

The everchanging branches of the world, the green
loves and the beautiful dark veins in time
must fall to lightnings and be calm in broken compassion:

but the wind moves outermost and hopeful
auguries: the strange opposition of a flower on a branch to
    its dark
wooden companion. On the gravel and the dry earth
each dry leaf is powder under the wheels   20
of war. But each brown root has protection
from the spike of flame. Each branch
tunnels to meet a well or inscrutable
history

shows the mortality of man
broken into scales that heal the strife of god.

The petals of space return
in a gnarled persistence like time.

To claim eternity as its own
time is this tree of the past   30
still grows from a mortal bosom.

So now when Hector dies, the creation of a hero
kills a father, a husband and all. What frail succession
    continues!

Why must he fall
when still a green branch

why shoulder a war with the sulky sky of god

To be truly mortal—
must Hector
to the immortal climb?

or to be truly fateful   40
to Hades lean before time
and be dusty and forgetful?

What glory has the almighty promised him?

only this—
capricious lightning of victory
while Achilles rests beside the ancient sea
while death waits in the guise of immortality.

Far off the clouds are tinged with pink and purple
the fire and darkness, the passion and the gloom of storm
the unearthly sense of valour subdued: but the caves of
     death   50
wait for the mortal
who turns in brightness to the immortal
blandishments of fame or fire!
the wild contest and the atrocious end
must dapple the world with flame and extinction
like still shadows moving in the memories of god.
Save for this tree that continues out of the breast of love,
shelter for what is beleaguered, the struggle that lives and
     shines!

So Hector knows the trunk of man, the branches of heroes
    and gods
foreshadowing the labour of all.   60

Loses his spear and groans to leave his love:
so is he pursued by a contradiction. The fine blades of grass
point their green arrows to his heart: the sun marches
to meet his young night,
his red flowers burning like inexorable stars: his roots serve
to change illusion and forsake
blossoming coals of immortal imperfection.

A. L. Hendriks/*Song for my brothers and cousins*

O what the heart has loved cannot be torn away!
The separate path, the lonely road is anguish, O my brothers,
for we are still in love, no matter what we say.

Lovers will hear no voice that tries to drive their love away
and what the heart once knows and loves, forever holds its
    sway:
our gentle cousins call us still in accents soft, my brothers,
for they are still in love, no matter what we say!

Islands of the south have much to share with us,
and much to give, and giving they are gay;

are we too poor to share our gifts with others? 10
are we so weak, so vain, so proud, my brothers?
and can the heart forget its promises, all in a single day?

The songs we sing will now lament this agonized delay,
but we are still in love, my brothers, no matter what we say,
and what the heart has loved, my brothers, cannot be torn
    away.

C. L. Herbert/*And the pouis sing*

In far days in happy shires
    In the perfumes that all day creep
From virgin mould, in the fires
Of a sullen but tolerant sun, deep,
        Our roots drilled deep and found
            In caverns underground
            Sweet water
        Rich as the laughter
That slept in Carib eye before fierce slaughter.
Through the soft air falling, 10
        Swifter than the sleek hawk dives
On the dove, on silent wing
Pilfered their caciques' lives
        At our feet in our shade
            Where once they had played
            In childhood
        Children of the sun
Who prayed to the sun to avenge their blood.

35

Hostile grew the sun and pitiless
    Spear sword arrow of light grew fiery   20
And in the blindness of their bitterness
Bored bird and beast and tree;
      Under the whip of savage winds
         And intricate with wounds
         Necrotic flesh
    Fell fold by fold from flanks
That never before had known the driver's lash.

Old, we are old before our prime
    (Springs of laughter ran dry
And hearts atrophied) and in our time   30
Have heard lips lift their cry
      To the stone-deaf skies, have seen
         How the hawk has been
         Stripped of pride
In necessary propitiation;
In vale on hill where slave and cacique died.

Have seen from the blood arise
    The cactus, live columbarium
Of the winged tears of indignant eyes,
And from its flowers come   40
      Dim odours, sweetening the air
         Through the desolate years
         And bringing
    To brittle, barren hearts
Auguries of new days, new faith, bright singing.

E. McG. Keane/*Rhapsody on a hill*

Come go
Scan the cut
Of the jig-saw clouds
Repatterning the sky

Watch knuckled showers
Bruising the light into rainbow

Catch the sun
Making eyes at the sea
The wind running
Blindfold over the mountains   10
Catching its breadth
In the deep valleys . . .

God is a child
And to-day I celebrate him

For not least in ecstasy
This life I walk that knifes me
This sun I love that slays me
    Beyond these green Ararats
Must breathe a dove
That does not need my sins   20
Nor search for
Perching on my callous limbs

For I am as young as heaven and Noah
With a new world to furnish
   I will build beauty like bird
And the bird will write his wing
Against the sun
   I will explain truth to the young sea
Sucking at the river's nipple

For here only I find   30
Mercy that has no mockery
And the sun intimate as a child's eye

What if here I dare kiss hands with time
Call God by his first name!
I have found God young and a fellow in these hills
And in this hour I do not bother with bleatings
My God the Father
Rather

        I turn and sing
        God the Child   40

For to-day I have walked
This nursery time
        And I have stumbled upon
        All the world's wheels and engines
        . . . and someone came running to me
        With the universe
        Like a top spinning in his hands . . .

E. McG. Keane/*Sourire*

I

Soon I shall watch
My last mountains queue up
For their share of horizon.
Soon make fast my eyes to a star
And no longer pretend
Not to have heard
The voice of the ocean's curled horn:
Book a wave for the world
A wave . . .
For the world, only a wave.   10

My God
Whoso taketh wings to fly dieth a little.

Oh when all I have tried to prove
Shall have become but a dry geometry of bones,
When they have laid me out cold
In a deep groove
And thrown dust in my eyes,
Will it ever be remembered
That once one who stood with his heels firm
On a firmly shifting deck,   20
Looked back at a host of waving eyes
And begged not for tears
But for prayers,
And wept at one world that proffered
Not an arrow, but a quiver of targets?

For the world, only a wave . . .

II

Strange that the ship moving anywhere
Shall seem to move nowhere.
Perhaps I shall stand idly by the rails
And look down into the deep cities of the sea,   30
Into the brown bulbous halls
Where blue freemasonries of whales move and mumble.

  At night I shall lose my eyes
  In the stark jungle of stars.
  Shall wonder of home,
Beneath how many moulds of change
Will they bury my last memory.

My God
Whoso taketh wings . . .

III

To-night, walking along the darkness   40
Where the sea's lips
Brush the wide smile of the bay lightly
And lightly again,
I think of the twenty-five tears the years have wept me,
Of the twenty-five meek errands I have run for time.
And oh strange that the ship moving anywhere
Shall seem to move nowhere . . .

My God, I would take wings of gladness
And die unto all worlds where no ships lie waiting,
Would grapple eyes to a star   50
And look where no mountains share the still horizon.

Yet mostly I shall remember my darkness
And the wide lips of the bay
Where the seas come lightly smiling,
And again lightly smiling.

George Lamming/*Dedication from Afar: A Song for Marian*

As fish slithering through unruffled pooks
Do not consider the water,
So you soaring in song
Our crumbling faiths recover.

Hearing as a boy the incredible fiction
Embroidering your name, I went this evening
Parading my colour for an auditorium's gaze
To autograph your fame, and to record
In language my desire no longer dictates
Your image in my song.   10

I cannot truly remember
Where memory and imagination meet,
Or sift the associations that cluster
And crowd the song we greet;

It may have been the music of feathered emissaries at
    carolling dawn,
Or the green lamb's threnody in a deepening chill;

It may have been the hum of sea at sundown,
Or the innocence of tears in the cradling years;
Or was it the voice of the river from which we climbed
Declaiming its limbs in alien lands?   20

      As fish hoisting their freedom
      Leap and are gone.
      So we at the second's command
      Met and were one.

Marian, gentlest of creatures from the darkest of continents,
What legacy can your art bestow
On these fortunate fools who marvel your excellence?
Or what grave terrors present
If love goes out of gear
And the darkest of continents explores its fear?   30

      Often in our green folly
      We mocked the celluloid display
      How darkies south of civilization
      Clowned their way to fame;

      And sometimes we laughed at tall tales
      Burgeoning from the deep dark south
      Or bade our understanding stand neutral;
      For the bulletins were so unreal.

      Now I venturing from scattered islands
      To rediscover my roots,   40
      Have found an impersonal city
      Where your tales are incredibly true;

And I who had never sworn violence
Nor charted courses for the heart's refusal
To white, black, brown, at home or afar,
Am urged to register with the outlaws.

Where under the sun is our shelter?
What meadow, stream or pool our ally?
What clocks shall register our waiting?
Or at midnight ripen our intentions?   50

To-day I decorate this song in sackcloth
For you and islands at anchor in the west,
And contemplate our criminals' love commandment:
Hate they brother as thyself.

George Lamming/*Swans*

By no other name are these
The imperturbable birds more beautiful,
No likelier image for the summer's curl
Of white light caught from the sea's
Arterial cells; or the moon's wry
Face carved on the curved aristocratic sky.

Sailing the solitude of their customary waters
Dark and dimpled, in the windy morning,
Instinct prompts a ritual of preening
The rude arrangement of their feathers,   10

And leaping with the leaping light of dawn
They crown the river with a white perfection.

Later the circus arrives
With its ready-made apparatus of pleasures,
Dogs and women and the dutiful masters
Of small boats swimming their lives
Through charted areas of water
And chuckled warnings of the wind's laughter.

The birds thoughtful, decorous, austere,
Retreat to a far side of the river,   20
Their eyes held in a puzzled stare
Measure their recently arrived spectator.
Some cluster to a deep deliberation
Or ponder in amazement their own reflection.

Leisurely the evening ambles,
Through the stained air, or torn leaves,
Over the lame, dry grasses,
Sadly, silently the late light falls,
And the waving curl of water dies
Where the winged white quietude at anchor lies.   30

Now blank desertion fills the senses,
Over the howling city
Louder than the cry of industry,
The moon sheds a contagion of madness,
And water fills the eyes of the visitor
Entering the legend of this historic river.

Walter MacA. Lawrence/*Futility*

The flowers are dead on the grave and a sad sight lay;
My token of love, you had thought and your heart had bled
As you laid them so tenderly there and behold in a day
The flowers are dead.

And as vain your love too long in the heart hid away.
Then, some of it shown in a smile or kind word said
Much more would have meant than tributes you now
     would pay—
The flowers are dead.

Walter MacA. Lawrence/*Kaieteur*

And falling in splendour sheer down from the height
    that should gladden the heart of an eagle to scan,—
That lend to the towering forest beside thee the semblance
    of shrubs trimmed and tended by man,—
That viewed from the brink where the vast amber volume
    that once was a stream cataracts into thee,
Impart to the foothills surrounding the maelstrom beneath
    thee that rage as the troublous sea,
The aspect of boulders that border a pool in the scheme of
    a rare ornamentalist's plan,
Where, where is the man that before thee is thrilled not—
    that scorneth the impulse to humble the knee,
With the scene of thy majesty resting upon him, and
    conscious of flouting some terrible ban?

Who, who can behold thee, O glorious Kaieteur, let down
    as it were from the fathomless blue,
A shimmering veil on the face of the mountain obscuring
    its flaws from inquisitive view,
Retouched with the soft, rosy glow of the morning and
    freaking the flow of desultory light,   10
Or bathed in the brilliant translucence of noontide a
    mystical mirror resplendently bright.
Or else in the warm sanguine glory of sunset, a curtain of
    gold with the crimsoning hue
Of the twilight upon it or drenched in the silvery flood of
    the moonlight subliming the night,
And feel not the slumbering spirit awaking to joy in the
    infinite greatly anew?

Ian McDonald/*Jaffo the Calypsonian*

Jaffo was a great calypsonian, a fire ate up his soul to sing and
    play calypso iron music.
Even when he was small he made many-coloured ping-pong
    drums and searched them for the island music,
Drums of beaten oil-barrel iron daubed in triangles with
    stolen paint from a harbour warehouse.
Now he seized the sorrow and the bawdy farce in metal-
    harsh beat and his own thick voice.
He was not famous in the tents: he went there once, and not
    a stone clapped, and he was afraid of respectable eyes:

The white-suited or gay-shirted lines of businessmen or
   tourists muffled his deep urge;
But he went back to the Indian tailor's shop and sang well,
   and to the Chinese sweet-and-sweepstake shop and
   sang well,
Unsponsored calypsoes; and in the scrap lots near the Dry
   River lit by one pitchoil lamp or two
He would pound his ping-pong and sing his hoarse voice out
   for ragged still-eyed men.
But in the rum-shop he was best; drinking the heavy sweet
   molasses rum he was better than any other calypso
   man.   10
In front of the rows of dark red bottles, in the cane-scented
   rooms his clogged throat rang and rang with staccato
   shout.
Drunk, then, he was best; easier in pain from the cancer in his
   throat but holding the memory of it.
On the rough floors of rum-shops strewn with bottle-tops and
   silver-headed corks and broken green bottle-glass
He was released from pain into remembered pain, and his
   thick voice rose and grated in brassy fear and fierce joke,
His voice beat with bitterness and fun as if he told of old things,
   hurt ancestral pride, and great slave humour.
He would get a rum if he sang well, so perhaps there was that
   of it too.
He was always the best, though, he was the best: the ragged
   men said so and the old men.
One month before he died his voice thickened to a hard
   final silence.
The look of unsung calypsoes stared in his eyes, a terrible
   thing to watch in the rat-trap rum-shops.

47

When he could not stand for pain he was taken to the public
    ward of the Colonial Hospital.   20
Rafeeq, the Indian man who in Marine Square watches the
    birds all day long for his God, was there also.
Later he told about Jaffo in a long mad chant to the rum-shop
    men. They laughed at the story:
Until the end Jaffo stole spoons from the harried nurses to
    beat out rhythm on his iron bedposts.

Basil McFarlane/*Ascension*

Carry me up some morning to the heights
Now that I have died.

Here among the stone piles have I died,
Here upon the sterile desert
Here by the cacti crucified.

Therefore carry me up some morning
To my father, I fulfilled;
Who is all knowledge and all strength
All wisdom and all fullness
All there is of truth   10
All green hills: I fulfilled.

Carry me up some morning.
Carry me up some morning to the heights
Where I shall live again
Supremely;
Where I have never died.

Basil McFarlane/*Jacob and the angel*

And shall a man, mortal
though the mind covets eternity, seek only
this seek only
to endure
whether failings of breath and bone, corruption
of flesh and faith?

Too thin too thin the wind
of consolation; here, the outer edge
of prayer, the unexorcized inexorcizable
knife self-knowledge   10

is closer to distant stars
whose stare
is lonely and unexplained, solemn and keen
unwinking like regret

than to old Earth, estranged now
a pillow of cold stone.

Basil McFarlane/*Letters to Margaret*

Yet how live if not by love
giver and gift
of life?

Faith, stern chisel
of our fortunes roots
in love is fuel is flame is
not to be confused with wishing.

Faith is learnt

Wishing mere reaction
to dull circumstance, projection   10
into infinite regions of the possible
of a finite will

So often a thoughtless rebel.

(3)

We have invented Fate
the turning world but not the mind
that sponsors its existence

feeble Mind

oh yet our single pride our one
and true inheritance:
possesses in its turn the earth and sky   20
invests dull earth
with wonder aims its noose
at the remotest of the glittering worlds.

(8)

Yet not without prayer is light
no light not song
and the song sacred:

A song is love the pure
emergent crystal of creative motion
is God who lays waste with terrible pity
our bright dark towers.   30

J. E. Clare McFarlane/*Sweet are the nights of May*

Sweet are the nights of May, the balmy nights
When crescent moons slant southward, and the stars
Glimmer from violet skies, and jasmine blooms
Scatter their fragrance over sleeping fields.
Sweetest to love, and youth's first taste of love,
The gold of moon-dreams and the silver sheen
Of dew-wet forest trees, and misty hills,
Dim and remote, lie unexplored desires
That rise in distant regions of the soul.

Sweet are the dawns of May, dew-moist and borne   10
Upon the odorous winds that nightly sleep
In flowery coverts, and at morn spread wide
Their wings before the day; where snowy mists,
From the lone peak diverging, nestle down,
Like curtains parted at the touch of Love,
To valleys deep below; and these to them
Pure joy and wonder were, whether beneath
The star-gemmed mantle of the night they roamed,
Or, standing on some wooded slope, beheld
The liquid sphere float free and pour its flood   20
Upon Cinchona's height.

Roger Mais/*I shall wait for the moon to rise*

I shall sit here and wait for the moon to rise,
And when she shall look at me,
From over the mountain-tops of tall bleak buildings
And come smiling down the valleys of the streets,
I shall ask her here to sit with me
In a Chinese tea garden under a divi-divi tree.

And a maiden golden like moon shall come
Wearing a clean white apron . . .
And I shall show her a bright new sixpence
And bid her shut her eyes   10
And paint with the pigments of all her dreams
The broad brave canvas of the skies.

And she will think: 'He is a little mad—
Decidedly he is a little mad.' . . .

I shall sit here and wait for the moon to rise.

Roger Mais/*Light love*

I, remembering how light love
hath a soft footfall, and fleet
that goes clicking down
the heart's lone

and empty street
in a kind
of spread twilight-nimbus of the mind,
and a soft voice of shaken laughter
like the wind . . .

I, remembering this,   10
And remembering that light love is
As fragile as a kiss
Lightly given,
And passes like the little rain
softly down-driven . . .

Bade love come to you
with rough male footsteps—
Deliberate—
That hurt to come,
And hurt to go . . .   20

And bade love speak to you
With accents terrible, and slow.

Una Marson/*Where death was kind*

Long had I thought
    Of death
And then they told me
You were dead.

I had seen him
Sitting in the ante-room
Eager to be summoned,
So when I heard
You had received him
I was silent.   10

I went to see you
Lying in death's embrace.
I was afraid—
I thought the sight
Would tear my heart
To pieces,
And my anger would rise
Against death the intruder.

But when I looked
Into your lovely face   20
And saw the sweet peace
That his kiss
Had implanted,
I could not weep,
And I could not be angry

Ah, sweet is death,
And kindly,
To those who suffer
Unbearable agony:
Sweet was death's kiss   30
Upon your lips—
Beloved one
To whom
He gave His Peace.

Leo (Egbert Martin)/*The swallow*

Who would not follow thee, swallow, in flight
On clean, swift wings thro' the opal light,
Away in purple of setting sun,
With a mad, wild joy till the day is done?
Who would not sweep, like a flash, thro' and thro'
The deep, vast void of the liquid blue,
With never a care but to cut the air,
With never a heed but delirious speed,
And a life—a full life indeed.

Who would not soar ever more and more,   10
Till the great earth seems but a spectre shore?
Who would not be in a sphere like thee,
Of glorious ether, for ever free?
Who would not mount with a swifter speed
Than the eye can follow or thought can heed;
With never a pause save to gently float,
On the sea of air like a drifting boat,
With a soft, full breast and a curving throat,

Past river and lake past the hills of white,
Past the houses' top at a dizzy height,   20
Past the silent lake thro' whose crystal breast
Thy faint shadow flits like a spiritual guest,
Past the low long lines of the great flat plains
Where eternal silence forever reigns,
So swiftly you fly now low and now high,
In chase with the clouds that lazily fly,
A voyager voyaging joyously.

Who would not follow thee, swallow, in flight,
In the cool, sweet air of the early night?
When each star hung high with its cheerful eye, 30
Drops golden treasure right gloriously,
And the moon high hung like a censer swung.
Floods a rare light ever fresh and young.
Oh, who would not follow thee, beautiful swallow,
From life and its trials so trying and hollow?
Who would not rise with a happy surprise
Away and away into happier skies?

Leo (Egbert Martin) *Twilight*

The twilight shuddered into gloom
The trees stood trembling in the air
And flung their green umbrageous arms
Above their wildly floating hair.

While saddened misereres fell
Like organ-peals in full excess
From breezes equal fall and swell
In agonies of bitterness.

The morning aged to older day
And burst in shreds of vivid light, 10
Bestrewing on the lying way
Its carnival of heat and light.

The wind a wondrous 'Gloria' rolled
Deep through the cloudy arch of space,
Chord after chord, whose notes of gold
Were smothered in the rhyme of grace.

Eric Roach/*Ballad of Canga*

Canga Brown is coming down
Stilted on his legend
Taller than a tall man,
Living beyond his end.

He is a old Ashantee man
Full of wickedness;
Bring obeah straight from Africa;
What he curse don't bless.

They gang him in the cane field;
Wouldn't raise a straw.   10
'Get up and work old man; look sharp.'
'Work is not for Canga.'

They tie him to the whipping post
In the greathouse yard
Big whip peeling off his back,
The missis bawling hard.

Canga working obeah bad,
Throwing all the pain
Hotter than he get it
On the baccra woman.   20

57

They let him go and chase him
To maroon in the bush.
'Go you worthless nigger,
Let hungry eat your flesh.'

But Canga go and sit down
By a tamarind tree,
Beat drum and call Damballa
Till his belly hungry.

He plant a plantain sucker,
Fill a tub with water,   30
Fish mullet from the water,
Cut plantain in one hour.

When moon go down old Canga
Put his skin in a jar,
Fly in a ball of fire;
Man turn soucouyan!

He suck the white man blood
Till his flesh come dry.
Only three days later
The man lay down and die.   40

He suck the baccra breeding sow
Till the hog come lean.
'Ent this hog was making pig?'
Everyone gone clean.'

What give Canga Brown that power?
He don't eat salt nor sugar;
His flesh fresh like Ibo yam,
His blood like clean rain water.

The devil come for Canga
Riding four black horses;   50
But Canga make black magic
And turn to two jackasses.

'Canga Brown! Ba Canga O!'
'Where the old man gone?'
Jackass braying loud like hell
Behind the baccra barn.

When God come for the man
And call him: 'Canga, Canga.'
That old sinner tie his mouth;
Not he, he wouldn't answer.   60

God stretch out his crookstick:
'Sinner, get up, go down,'
'Lord, call me Mister Brown.'

God vex until he laugh in heaven;
Pull a big chair for Canga.
Is that why when the man dead
You hearing so much thunder.

Eric Roach/*To my mother*

It is not long, not many days are left
Of the dead sun, nights of the crumbled moon;

Nor far to go; not all your roads of growth,
Love, grief, labour of birth and bone
And the slow slope from the blood's noon
Are shorter than this last.

And it is nothing. Only the lusty heroes
And those whose summer's sweet with lust
And wine and roses fear. The children do not;
Theirs is young Adam's innocence.   10
The old do not; they welcome the earth's suction
And the bone's extinction into rock.

The image of your beauty growing green,
Your bone's adolescence I could not know,
Come of your middle years, your July loins.
I found you strong and tough as guava scrub,
Hoeing the growing, reaping the ripe corn;
Kneading and thumping the thick dough for bread.

And now you're bowed, bent over to the ground;
An old gnarled tree, all her bows drooped   20
Upon the cross of death, you crawl up
Your broken stairs like Golgotha, and dead bones
Clutch at your dying bones . . .

I do not mourn, but all my love
Praise life's revival through the eternal year.
I see death broken at each seed's rebirth.
My poems labour from your blood
As all my mind burns on our peasant stock
That cannot be consumed till time is killed.

Oh, time's run past the time your hands made bread
To this decrepitude; but in the stream
Of time I watch the stone, the image
Of my mother making bread my boyhood long,
Mossed by the crusty memories of bread.
O may my art grow whole as her hands' craft.

W. Adolphe Roberts/*Villanelle of the living Pan*

Pan is not dead, but sleeping in the brake,
     Hard by the blue of some Ægean shore.
Ah, flute to him, Beloved, he will wake.

Vine leaves have drifted o'er him flake by flake
     And with dry laurel he is covered o'er.
Pan is not dead, but sleeping in the brake.

The music that his own cicadas make
     Comes to him faintly, like forgotten lore,
Ah, flute to him, Beloved, he will wake.

Let not the enemies of Beauty take   10
     Unction of Soul that he can rise no more.
Pan is not dead but sleeping in the brake,

Dreaming of one that for the goat god's sake
     Shall pipe old tunes and worship as of yore.
Ah, flute to him, Beloved, he will wake.

So once again the Attic coast shall shake
        With a cry greater than it heard before:
'Pan is not dead, but sleeping in the brake!'
        Ah, flute to him, Beloved, he will wake.

A. J. Seymour/*Sun is a shapely fire*

I
Sun is a shapely fire turning in air
Led by white springs
            and earth's a powerless sun.

I have the sun to-day deep in my bones.
Sun's in my blood, light heaps beneath my skin.
Sun is a badge of power pouring in
A darkening star that rains its glory down.

The trees and I are cousins. Those tall trees
That tier their branches in the hollow sky
And, high up, hold small swaying hands of leaves
Up to divinity, their name for sun,   10
And sometimes mine. We're cousins.

Sheet light, white power comes falling through the air,
—All the light here is equal-vertical—
Plays magic with green leaves and, touching, wakes
   The small sweet springs of breathing scent and bloom
That break out on the boughs.

And sun has made
Civilization flower from a river's mud
With his gossamer rays of steel.

II

These regions wear sharp shadows from deep suns.   20

The sun gives back her earth its ancient right
The gift of violence.

Life here is ringed with the half of the sun's wheel
And limbs and passions grow in leaps of power
Suddenly flowing up to touch the arc.

Upon this energy kin to the sun
To learn the trick of discipline and slow skill,
Squaring in towns upon an empty map
Hitching rivers to great water wheels,
Taming the fire to domesticity.   30

III

Sun is a shapely fire floating in air
Watched by God's eye. The distance makes it cool
With the slow circling retinue of worlds
Hanging upon it.
          Indifferently near
Move other stars with their attendant groups
Keeping and breaking pace in the afternoon
Till the enormous ballet music fades
And dies away.

Sun is a shapely fire   40
Turning in air
Sun's in my blood.

Philip M. Sherlock/*A beauty too of twisted trees*

A beauty too of twisted trees
The harsh insistence of the wind
Writes lines of loveliness within
The being of this tortured trunk.
I know that some there are that spring
In effortless perfection still,
No beauty there of twisted trees
Of broken branch and tortured trunk
And knotted root that thrusts its way
Impatient of the clinging clay.   10

John who leapt in the womb has fled
Into the desert to waken the dead,
His naked body broken and torn
Knows nothing now of Bethlehem's peace,
And wild of mood and fierce of face
He strives alone in that lonely place.
Ezekiel too saw the dry bones live
The flames and smoke and conflict give
A lightning flash to the dead man's sight
And Moses smote the rock, no rock   20
In a weary cactus-land to mock
Hollow men stuffed with straw, but a rock
That freely pours from its riven side
Water for those who else had died . . .

And hangs on a twisted tree
A broken body for those who see,

All the world, for those who see
Hangs its hope on a twisted tree.
And the broken branch and the tortured trunk
Are the stubborn evidence of growth   30
And record proud of strife, of life.

A beauty too of twisted trees.

Philip M. Sherlock/*Pocomania*

Long Mountain, rise,
Lift you' shoulder, blot the moon.
Black the stars, hide the skies,
Long Mountain, rise, lift you' shoulder high.

Black of skin and white of gown
Black of night and candle light
White against the black of trees
And altar white against the gloom,
Black of mountain high up there
Long Mountain, rise,   10
Lift you' shoulder, blot the moon,
Black the stars, black the sky.

Africa among the trees
Asia with her mysteries
Weaving white in flowing gown
Black Long Mountain looking down
Sees the shepherd and his flock
Dance and sing and wisdom mock,

Dance and sing and falls away
All the civilized to-day 20
Dance and sing and fears let loose;
Here the ancient gods that choose
Man for victim, man for hate
Man for sacrifice to fate
Hate and fear and madness black
Dance before the altar white
Comes the circle closer still
Shepherd weave your pattern old
Africa among the trees
Asia with her mysteries. 30

Black of night and white of gown
White of altar, black of trees
'Swing de circle wide again
Fall and cry me sister now
Let de spirit come again
Fling away de flesh an' bone
Let de spirit have a home.'

Grunting low and in the dark
White of gown and circling dance
Gone to-day and all control 40
Now the dead are in control
Power of the past returns
Africa among the trees
Asia with her mysteries.

Black the stars, hide the sky
Lift you' shoulder, blot the moon.
Long Mountain rise.

Philip M. Sherlock/*Trees his testament*

A GOODBYE FOR DALEY

Daley's dead; dust now, gone for good
Far over Jordan side
Left his body this side
Of the cold river.
Dead now, gone for good
Nobody see him till Kingdom come
And the trumpet call beyond the river
And the roll call.
Gone for good,
Lips greedy once for a woman's breast   10
Still now and silent
Pasture for the worm
Then dust.

Daley was a plumber,
Served his time to Hard Up,
Hungry Belly walked beside him
Never left him quiet
Through the slum he had for home
From door to door he asked
If they wanted toilets fixed   20
And they laughed for the toilet wasn't theirs anyway.
Walked and tramped from door to door
Raising cash for peace of mind,
Pocket full is belly full
Belly full is peace of mind.

Hungry Belly never left him,
Grinned and gnawed and never left him
Who would mend what wasn't his anyway?
Plumber's dead now, gone for good.
Daley's dead.   30

Hungry Belly restless talked
When he saw his Daley buy
Paint and canvas for a picture
For a picture when a plumber had to live.
But the painter was a-seeking
For the something that he couldn't tell about
That he knew inside he must search and search and find.
Knock and knock until he find

Past the questions and divisions
Past the doubtings and the troubles   40
Past the doors and rows of doors
Till at last he saw it all in the trees;
They were quiet and at peace in the pastures
And beside the waters still
And upon the mountain side
Where the drought would parch the roots
And the hurricane would walk in the Summer,
Trunks and roots were hard and torn
Branches broken short, and twisted,
Just to keep a footing there   50
Just to be a living tree.
Plumber's hand and painter's eye,
Plumber's dead and gone for good,
Daley's dead.

Over now the search for silver
Gone away is Hungry Belly
Off to find a fresh companion;
Dust the feet that walked beside him,
Turned to dust the plumber's hands
But the trees still stand together   60
Like they're shouting over Jordan,
And, look see how cedar trees
Do shade a garden in that place.
And upon that skull-shaped hill top
When the eye of day is clean
Stand two trees with bitter bearing
And between the two a tree
One between the two that lifts
Bright flowering.

M. G. Smith/*Mellow oboe*

The wind breathes a mellow oboe in my ear
I from the seas of life
Have filled my cup with foam.

The tension of Time's waves has broken on
These cliffs
The menace is resolved in foam.

O beautiful
O beautiful
The cruelty.

Soon the suave night's surrender
And the mass music of the dark
Falls fragment into foam.

To apprehend the foam the waves declared
And drink the milk pure from the farm of Time.

Nebular and luminous
The stars the peaks achieve
Found foam of peaks and stars.

So bracket the stars with bubble
Fill baskets of white berries from the sea
All is a rich donation
The waves are lines of epic
The sea a deep quotation
The foam the complete poem.

I hear the sea's half-breath half-moan
Sweep in fugues through me
And the wind breathes an oboe in my ear.

M. G. Smith/*The vision comes and goes*

The vision comes and goes
Light does not last
Nor yields the tropic night
That swims with stars
A clearer insight that this furtive mist
Nor gives the sun more flaming truth than snows

Let the wind walk
Where the wind will
Let the streams flow
Where the sea calls
The crags and trees
Sprung from the hill
Are buds and stalks
Of all the vision
Wind would know
And water leaping from the falls.

Circle us endlessly
Spin wheel and dance
Touch that is destiny
Touch that is chance
Who shall deliver
Infinite, free
Which wind will tame thee
Boundless past dream
Into what distance
Travels the stream?

Not all the stars
Nor suns
Nor dreams so bright
Nor all the heavens
Quivering with day
Attain the purpose
Or reflect the light
Each is a shadow
Let fall on thy way

Inward and outward
To create and show
Faith
Where the darkness obliterates all form
Faith like a river   40
Down which all life must flow
Faith
Like the rainbow
Encircling storm on storm.

O lonely Spirit
Wandering through the glades
Sensed
Near in mountains
Music
And with friends   50
Glimpsed
And lost sight of
Felt and never known
Long is thine absence
Bruised
Torn—
Thick with shades
Blind
All about us
Yet here where reason ends   60
Come
Enter gently
Possess
And make thy home.

Harold M. Telemaque/*Poem*

To those
Who lifted into shape
The huge stones of the pyramid;
Who formed the Sphinx in the desert,
And bid it
Look down upon the centuries like yesterday;
Who walked lithely
On the banks of the Congo,
And heard the deep rolling moan
Of the Niger;   10
And morning and evening
Hit the brave trail of the forest
With the lion and the elephant;
To those
Who, when it came that they should leave
Their urns of History behind,
Left only with a sad song in their hearts;
And burst forth into a soulful singing
As bloody pains of toil
Strained like a hawser at their hearts   20
To those, hail . . .

Harold M. Telemaque/*Roots*

Who danced Saturday mornings
Between immortelle roots,
And played about his palate
The mellowness of cocoa beans.

Who felt the hint of the cool river,
In his blood,
The hint of the cool river
Chill and sweet.

Who followed curved shores
Between two seasons.
Who took stones in his hands
Stones white as milk.
Examining the island in his hands;
And shells,
Shells as pink as frog's eyes
From the sea.

Who saw the young corn sprout
With April rain.
Who measured the young meaning
By looking at the moon.
And walked roads a footpath's width,
And calling,
Cooed with mountain doves
Come morning time.

Who breathed mango odour
From his polished cheek.
Who followed the cus-cus weeders
In their rich performance.
Who heard the bamboo flute wailing
Fluting, wailing,
And watched the poui golden
Listening.

Who with the climbing sinews
Climbed the palm
To where the wind plays most,
And saw a chasmed pilgrimage
Making agreement for his clean return.
Whose heaviness
Was heaviness of dreams,
From drowsy gifts.   40

Derek Walcott/*A city's death by fire*

After that hot gospeller had levelled all but the churched sky,
I wrote the tale by tallow of a city's death by fire.
Under a candle's eye that smoked in tears, I
Wanted to tell in more than wax of faiths that were snapped
     like wire.

All day I walked abroad among the rubbled tales.
Shocked at each wall that stood on the street like a liar,
Loud was the bird-rocked sky, and all the clouds were bales
Torn open by looting and white in spite of the fire;

By the smoking sea, where Christ walked, I asked why
Should a man wax tears when his wooden world fails.   10

In town leaves were paper, but the hills were a flock of faiths
To a boy who walked all day, each leaf was a green breath

Rebuilding a love I thought was dead as nails,
Blessing the death and the baptism by fire.

Derek Walcott/*The yellow cemetery*

'They are alive and well somewhere
The smallest sprout shows there is really no death
And if ever there was it led forward life, and does not wait at
 the end to arrest it.'

WALT WHITMAN

I

All grains are the ash to ashes drowsing in the morning,
Wearing white stone. I passed them, not thankfuller to be
Their living witness, not noisy in salt like the near sea,
Because they are spaded to the dirt, our drowning.
As lovely as the living, and safer, to the bay's green mourners
They will unkeening bones, and they are happy.
Lost the candle and censer mysterytale, the swung smoke of
 adorners
Of dying; Could they speak more than bramble, they'd be
One in the language of the sun and the bibleling froth.
Their now bread is broken stone, their wine the absent blood 10
They gave to days of nails.
                              It is enough
And greater is no grace, no surplice more serviceable than
 the lap and hood
Of the seasons that grew them, and now mother them to sleep.
And you alive, speak not of the unlucky dead, the sunless
 eyes rotten
Under down and saddles in a kingdom of worms.
Speak of the luckless living, that are gnawed by a misbegotten
Moon and memory;

It is a blessing past bounds to miss the dooms
Of the vertical fathom, at each suncrow   20
To know no anguish, cool in clothstones that flow,
The sleep in the bone, all weathers.
                                    But we, each
Flapping boast of the crowing sun, turn in our linen graves,
Face stale mornings, old faces, but these dead on the beach
Are joyed at the dawn's blood skyed on their dearth of days.
We cocky populations fouling the fallow plans of heaven,
Shall find perfection in a cemetery under a hill.
For we have suffered so long, that death shall make all even,
There shall the love grow again that once we would kill. 30
This is no place for the eater of herbs and honey for beads,
Here are water, crops, seabirds, and yet here do not be brave,
Seek no fames, and do not too often pray to keep alive,
Against the brittle wick of wishes the wind in the clock strives
And wins. Was not your father such?
Gay in the burning faith of himself, but melted to forgetting?
Thank time for joys, but be not thankful overmuch,
The sun a clot of the wounded sky is setting.
Delve no heart in the sound of your soul, a man's speech burns
And is over; the tears melt, colden and stales the tallow. 40
And the story of your ash to ashes breath that the wind learns,
The bushes from your eyes will tell in a deeper yellow.

II

And there at sea, under the wave,
The sea-dead, the legendary brave,
Under the windmaned horses of the sea
Float the bulged trampled dead, nudged by whales;

77

Their wicks windkilled too, by salty gales,
And they were so braver, less alarmed than we.
For we want to run, who do not want to drown where
There is no angel or angelus or another's helphand;   50
But they too ride easy and the nunnery of brown hair
Of the white girl of walls, shall be no more in the pardoner
    sand
Black man's denial. Heart, let us love all, the weeds
That feed the sea-herds, miracler than man's tallest deeds,
For here the living are blinder than the dead, ah
Look a rainbow sevencoloured wakes glory through the
    clouds and
Breasts sea and hill and cemetery in warning,
And the chained horses thunder white, no more adorning
The harbour that grows truculent at the sevenhued sky,
A canoe scuds home quickly, and indigo reigns.   60
Praise these but ask no more the meaning of mourning.
Than you ask a moral from the seven glory of the clouds, and
Go slowly to the hill as the gale breaks, crazy on the loud
    sand
Do not talk of dying, you say, but all men are dead or sick,
In the brain and rib-hollow rooms
The candles of the eye burn and shorten, and how quick
The fine girl sleeps in her grave of hair, the grasshair
    tombs,
O look at the sane low populations of the democratic dead,
How all are doomed to a dome of mud, all brought to book,
Believing in a world for the perverse saint and the holy crook. 70

Love children now, for the sun will batter their thinklessness
    away,

For there, if place, He walks, who was a lifelong child,
And when the sun is spearing them in growth, pray,
There is the kingdom of haven in the tears of a child.
The trees, alive in a wind of generations, spin a terror of
    grains
In the air, in the blue and froth of the weather, the branch
    rains
Yellow on the graves.

        We, the raisers of a God against the hand,
Wonder who is made or maker, for the God our ancestors
    learned
Moses of terror, burns in no bushes,   80
We pray only when seas are turned
Angry, and the wild wind rushes,
And love and death we cannot understand.
The signatures of a lost Heaven remain,
The beauty of the arch, the nature not sun not rain
We want our God to be. And yet were He scanned
We the long builders of beyond this flying breath would
    look
Beyond the written Heavens, the wide open sea, the land
    like a green book.
Would find the Author and the Author's purpose.

III

A swallow falls, and perhaps the sole spoken prayer   90
Is the hand of a leaf crossing the cold curled claws.
Where is the God of the swallows, is He where
Lives the one whom you flew young from, who all life was
    yours?

And yet for all these gifts, the gift that I can pray,
The mountain music, the pylon words, the painting, they are
Enough, and may be all, for they add grace by day
And night give tears as harshly as a telling star.
Were there nothing, and this the only
Life, a man has still to save the cliche of his soul, to live
With, I will say it, grace to atone for the   100
Sins that all the worlds awoke before he ailed alive,
Climb there, go to the hill where another Sun is warning,
That the wicks weaken and in the halls of the heartsun, love,
For love is the stone speech that outlasts our ash and mourning.

Daniel Williams/*Over here*

Over here where our islands
Puncture the leaden sea into a chain,
And our wish inconstant like the pilloried
Sun fatigued by clouds, here where pain
Is narcotic, blunt and dull, frenzied
We have hoped.

Not for the nurturing of a million
Varied wish or the relish of a lotus
Pleasure; not for the temporary brazen
Triumph the coin has taught or the sick   10
Culture which understands only the voice
Of duped builders.

Rather the ubiquitous call of the river
For the salt panting of the sea, rather
The proud turn of the leaf's neck
For the hot kiss of the sun and the weak
Reach of the hand for the strong grasp
Of the comrade.

For here we have loved
The wet mud clinging to the hoemen's feet.   20
Here in the soil our blood is green and
In our wine the vine is parched with the
Heat or our hope; yet untamed is the spark
Of desire, strong in young strength.

Time reaches for the harp
Of history, and in the east dawn brings
Her dower of light and flings it to her
Husband day; glance in the west, the golden
Egg will break into myriad suns and people
Our horizon.   30

Look at the land, the psalms,
Singing for our sons beyond the fever of the years;
Look at the trees, the prayers,
Curtseying before the sacred scribbling of the wind,
And the clouds the white precipitate of the sky
Like incense on the altar.

Notes

THESE critical notes are only intended as a guide. They represent one person's approach towards the understanding of these poems and must not be taken as the 'right' answers. Although in some cases the poets have helped with certain facts, it does not even follow that even *they* are necessarily right. The poem is its own justification and the intelligent reader will return time and time again to the poem itself to discover new points of significance, to verify, to disagree. 'Explanations' are always suspicious anyway, for they suggest that the poem lacked something for which the trite prose of everyday wear can be a substitute. If these notes serve to stimulate discussion, the efforts of the editor will have been adequately rewarded.

DAWN IS A FISHERMAN/*page* 16
There is an attempt here to link the activities and qualities of dawn. The effect of the poem is made by the subtle juxtaposing of images closely associated with one another. This is the basic technique, and prevents the poem from being merely an equation between dawn and the natural world. The coming morning is expressed in human terms—'dawn is a fisherman' and the sun is 'a bare foot boy'. Associated with this is the waking world described appropriately in human terms—darkness is said to squat, the houses 'peep at the stars' and the cocks crow 'like city trumpeters'. The human link reaches completeness in the last four lines which gather the meaning and extend the rhythm into a grand, rather anthem-like finale.

1. *harpoon:* used for catching whales. The point here is that just as men throw a harpoon to catch whales, so dawn throws light to catch the darkness.
9. *hurtle:* a clumsy way of describing the speed of the birds.
10. *self-criticized auditions:* the birds sound as if they are singing to one another, each one trying to better the other. But here the phrase is much too pompous for the poem.

THERE IS A MYSTIC SPLENDOUR/*page* 16
This poem is much more personal than the previous one. There is also a note of patriotism which is not overdone. The poet attempts to recapture history in a moment of time. This history is to do with pirates, and it seems to the poet that the sounds of the wave are like battles cries, and the palm trees reminiscent of buried treasure. Despite the historical association, the poem does not quite succeed, since events are never elevated above the sensational.
3. *keel:* the part of a ship running along the bottom from stem to stern and supporting the entire frame.
4. *beached and drawn:* anchored at the beach.
6. *Bay:* a reference to the Bay of Honduras, at one time the haunt of pirates.
8. *sickle isle:* Halfmoon Caye, an island off the coast of British Honduras, shaped like a sickle.
10. *predatory:* those who live by plunder.
    Brethren of the Coast: this refers to the Buccaneers who in the seventeenth century harassed shipping from their various bases.
16. *Captain Morgan* (c. 1635–1688) was a famous buccaneer of the day and it is believed that some of his treasure was buried in Halfmoon Caye. He was afterwards made a deputy Governor of Jamaica.

Vera Bell re-evaluates her own place as a Negro in the history of the West Indies. By the repetition of 'ancestor on the auction block', she emphasizes the humiliation of the slave. The poem describes a dramatic re-assessment of self; the third stanza of the poem marks the turning point towards the new understanding. Intentionally the rhythm of the first two stanzas is fixed, almost harsh, and the lines contract into disappointing revelations at the end. But the last two stanzas re-build the faith in herself, a faith which comes about through new understanding; this is why there is an expansive pattern in these lines.

Because she is dealing with an emotional situation, it is a little difficult to judge the poem. Certainly parts of it seem like histrionic gestures, others a trifle illogical and the end is far too public to be good poetry. Finally, however, one is left with a deep feeling of satisfaction and awe, partly derived from an insistent belief in the future.

5. *primitive:* here used in a derogatory sense to suggest a former attitude to her slave-past.
19. *eternal abyss:* death; hell; the absence of any tradition in her life. This, because of its religious connotation, introduces the Christian link which binds her to her slave ancestor.

HISTORY MAKERS/*page* 19
In much the same way that Vera Bell protested, so does George Campbell in this poem. But because it is more direct and because it does not strike attitudes, it is more successful. The language is stripped to the barest minimum, rhythm is reduced to its most primitive form; therefore one's attention is directed solely at the road-side women breaking rocks to help mend the roads. Their monotonous occupation comes

over in the repetition of lines and words, in the obvious rhyme and in the way that the poem seems to describe a complete circle and return to its own beginning. Some of the words seem to conjure up a world of associations—'haphazard frocks' followed later on by 'pregnant frocks', suggest both their poverty and their role as child bearers.

3. *child makers:* the dialect helps emphasize the important part that these women have played.

12-14. *No smiles/No sigh/No moan:* the women have been forced to become as unfeeling as the rocks.

18. *destiny shapers:* they help build the future.

LITANY/*page* 20

A deceptively simple poem which has the tone of a prayer. From the first line until the penultimate, each successive image builds on the other until the nature allusions add up to a religious statement. Lines 4-11 remind one of the statement and response of church liturgy.

5. *poinsettia:* small greenish yellow flowers surrounded by scarlet floral leaves. They usually bud at Christmas in the West Indies.

6. *cassia:* a purple and yellow flowering tree.

OH! YOU BUILD A HOUSE/*page* 21

A man building a house, a pregnant woman, a father rearing a family and God creating the universe, are all compared here. The poet feels that they are all one and the same process of creation, and in its quiet tone the poem seeks to emphasize the link between them all. This is a very didactic poem but to a large extent the didacticism is hidden by the sober and firm quality of the thought. But at the centre of the poem there is always the significant act of building a house; in the first stanza it is associated with conception, in the second with rearing a family. In other words there has been progression of the child image, from womb to childhood. This is firmly linked in the third stanza with the child's dream, which far outstrips man's most ambitious creation. The 'yet' of the fourth stanza is important; it emphasizes man's limitations and the earlier theme of building a house; man cannot create anything greater than himself—it is almost futile to want to build. The process of building becomes therefore an endless attempt at starting over and over again; the child image of the fifth stanza which takes one back to the first illustrates this. The builder has become like a mother, and like her, his truest expression must be a turning inwards. At the end, the poem says that all personal creation is a way of understanding the significance of life and people—'the journey through one to the world of men'. The sky, which in stanza two could not be constructed, is resurrected in the last stanza and building comes to mean a link with the ultimate creativity of God and a way of safeguarding one's peace. For Campbell peace is used in a secular and religious sense—in other words the peace of mind and the peace of God.

'Oh! You Build a House' is a religious poem in the widest meaning of the word, in that it seeks to come to terms with the significance of all human effort. Throughout the poem the quiet, almost apologetic, tone is in keeping with the theme. The stanzas seem to be groping their way towards elucidation, and they become longer and more expansive as the poem develops. Part of the cumulative effect is achieved by the repetition of words and phrases, and by an obvious use of parallelism. What is perhaps more subtle is the use and re-use of certain basic images and phrases in the poem, which accumulate meaning as they are repeated.

5. *The whole . . . creating:* the woman's entire life is occupied with her child-bearing.
8. *wilfully:* with care, knowing what they want them to be.

12–14. *Where are . . . would dream:* is there anyone who can create the ideals in the mind of a child?

19–21. *mad like a man . . . peace in his face:* he has seen the limitations of his own powers.

27–29. *Here is the reconstruction . . . his own infiniteness:* as one creates one realizes that true peace is not external but within; creating is a way of discovering one's capacity.

39. *The journey through one to the world of men:* through a re-discovery of one's self, one can come to a better understanding of what people ere.

41. The images here suggest the chaos of the external world.

UNIVERSITY OF HUNGER/*page 23*

This is one of Martin Carter's best known poems and takes a long-term historical view of the meaning and significance of the suffering of the ordinary man. It begins with a series of surrealistic statements which suggest the way in which the world is seen by such people. Then the poet attempts to look at the people himself and comes up with the same viewpoint, emphasizing their destitution and misery. These two viewpoints are complementary in the poem—the first introduced by 'is', demonstrates the loss (the sentences are without a subject), and the second introduced by 'they come', re-instates the plight in a sinister way. The poet notes the disfiguration that has taken place in people since they could be sure of nothing; they have 'metal brows' and 'the golden moon like a big coin' is a symbol of this dehumaniza-tion. The importance given to 'wide is the span' further emphasizes this point; they can never really become men because they have been degraded by the consequences of the system into which they were born.

Appropriately the poem adopts a mournful note with long open vowels which help to prolong the lines. This type of theme could easily degenerate into a long pointless moan but it is saved from this by the nature images (startlingly out of place), and by the vitality of some of the symbols. There are also certain lines which suggest a great deal in their crisp fashion—'the bearded men fall down and go to sleep' for instance, is almost like a child's observation of death. Certain labels do not function well in the poem—'the terror and the time', 'the cruel wind blowing'; being mere hackneyed phrases they do little to develop the subject. But on the whole since the poem depends for its final effect on a process of selective listing, the poet has set himself a very difficult task. He fails in the sixth stanza but this is ably compensated for in the others.

1. *university of hunger:* men learn to live through suffering.
5. *the plains of life . . . in spasms:* life, for the suffering, seems spasmodic and full of vicissitudes. Compare lines 16–17.
7. *treading in the hoofmarks of the mule:* it is a symbol of their degradation that the mule boys have to follow the mules.
13. *middle air to middle earth:* from one uncertainty to another.
15. Note *bars* and *metal* which suggest both their anger and their dehumanization.
35. *the flood of bone beneath the floor of flesh:* a reference to death. They die and they seem to be continually dying.
43. *in the torture of sunset in purple bandages:* this suggests the agony that they endure.
54. *shell blow:* a shell was blown to summon estate labourers to work.
   iron clang: the iron clasps used on the hands and feet of slaves.

BENEATH THE CASUARINAS/*page 25*
Two people walking underneath casuarinas provide the departure point for this mystical experience. The poet does

not try to explain what happens—he points out the silence and the unreality of the environment. Then come various suggestions of what the experience probably is—the use of 'might', the alternatives which follow 'or' and the final question mark; one is prepared for the statement 'we shall never know'.

1. *casuarinas:* tall feathery trees with jointed leafless branches. They bear a corn-shaped seed and are found all over Barbados. It is called the 'mile tree' in Guyana and 'weeping willow' in Jamaica.

5-6. *Overhead the casuarinas . . . poised for flight:* the leaves of the tree seem like feathers which are about to float away but cannot.

10. *desolate tides:* a seashore without water.

14-16. *It is the beat . . . midday heat:* in the experience it seems that tree and person become one.

18-21. A series of impressions of the sea.

21-22. *silence made manifest in sound:* everything was perfectly still until the inexplicable sound came: the sound of the rustling leaves contrast with the previous silence.

HYMN TO THE SEA/*page* 26

A praise poem to the sea; each stanza is devoted to a different aspect of the significance of the sea—the sensual, the physical, the spiritual, the imaginative and the procreative. The first stanza shows how the senses respond to the sea; there is a delicate touch here—the sea is almost nymph-like. The harsher sounds in the next stanza describe the physical nature, and the 'embracing womb' of the third stanza confirms the significance of the view the poet takes. The penultimate stanza introduces the idea of fecundity to which the poet will return in the last.

10. *crisscrossed with stillness:* a description of the ripples on a calm day.

11. *windruffed:* made uneven by the wind.

12. *Titans:* giants who fought against Zeus. The poet is suggesting that the waves can be high.

14. *breakwater:* stones erected to break the force of waves.

20. *saltfruit:* anything that the sea produces—particularly small cocoanut-shaped objects and sea-weed with tiny berries.

35. *once a goddess arose:* a reference to Aphrodite who was born from the sea-foam.

30–31. *the patterning . . . musing mind:* a contemplative human mind can only hope to copy the regularity of ebb and flow.

37. *her signature:* Barbados is a coral island.

39. *red roofs:* red roofed houses.
    her blue: the blue of the sea.

RETURN/*page 28*

Here the poet takes up a theme which was the climax of 'Hymn to the Sea': the sea is responsible for all life. The majestic achievements of the sea are emphasized in contrast to the ordinary accomplishments of man. The memory of the sea has persisted always in man's very self and it is to the sea that he will return.

Part of the effect of this poem, like the previous one, arises from repetition; here 'we shall come down to the sea' is repeated in two stanzas and the variation in the third with the pun 'see' is most effective.

3. *lichened:* covered with lichens.

3–4. *rust/Stains the stone:* the crusts and tufts formed by the lichen and stones.

6. *leviathan:* a huge sea-monster.

7. *wrack:* destruction, an old-fashioned word which conveys the idea of the antiquity of the ruins.

17. *coronals:* the waves seem to have designed small crowns in the sand; they signify recognition by the sea of man's small achievements and welcome him back to the sea.

BIRTH IS . . ./*page* 29

Physical birth, the poet suggests ironically, makes us endure too much; human beings are not prepared for suffering and therefore never experience love. As a result our relationships with one another suffer for we have not come to any genuine understanding through experiencing agony together. There are overtones in the poems of the crucifixion of Christ; the poet thinks that human beings are incapable even of a small imitation of it. Although there is never an overt moral statement, the poet suggests that life has to be looked at in a realistic manner and that the people who feel that they are in charge of their own destinies and those of others, should know that they are wrong.

Short clipped statements help to contribute to the effect of the sonnet, as well as occasional onomatopoeia and forceful paradox. The dry style is in keeping with the very serious and logical argument; very different poetry since here it is the intellect at work, in contrast with the second poem where one is back in the familiar West Indian world of landscape effusions.

1. *Birth is too bloody:* physical birth is too difficult for humans. They would prefer to be born without pain.
   the end: all that happens after birth up to the time of death.
4. *perfumed path:* life seems to be full of ease.
5. *unknown friend:* all relationships take time to develop and usually come out best at a time of crisis.
6. *agony of mother and child:* this refers of course not only to our own immediate world but to Mary and Christ.

7. *we are solicicitous:* contrary to the Bible injunction which compares our lot to the lilies of the field. References like this make the poem a sermon in verse.

10–11. *Suppose our seed . . . temerity:* if we did think of posterity we would realize that it was necessary to be involved in agony.

12–13. *throes like waves . . . final verity:* suppose pain were to destroy our cherished illusions about ourselves and make us see the truth, that we are not everything.

14. *infinite shores:* we realize the vastness of the universe; beyond are powers far greater than us.

OEDIPUS AT COLONUS/*page* 29

The story of Oedipus is told in three plays by Sophocles: the words of the oracle came true and Oedipus killed his father and married his mother. He then blinded himself and set out with his two daughters; finally he goes into a grove to die. The poem begins at the end and the details of his life are filled in by a series of flashbacks. The whole poem is marked by a tone of quiet resignation and contrasting colours—light and dark, black and white—help focus one's attention on the nature of the experience that Oedipus is about to undergo. The poem takes the reader forward in time and Oedipus's reflections about past and future help syncretize all time; at the beginning he has just arrived at the grove; at the end he is about to follow the setting sun towards his own death.

1. *mountains:* They suggest Oedipus's longing for death and for purity. It is more than possible that the poet was describing the mountains of his native Jamaica.

6. *at dawn to wait for dusk:* while I am still alive to wait for my death.

7. *life-giver:* both the sun and God.

8. *silver lace of dew:* a rather overdone comparison. The poet is contrasting the early morning outside and the darkness of the grove within.

10. *After noon he will withdraw:* as the sun declines so does Oedipus's life.

15. *him:* the life-giver. Oedipus goes to his death (the dark) by (paradoxically) following the life-giver.

17. *daughters:* Antigone and Ismene.

19. *day-tramp:* the disaster which has been his life.

CANES BY THE ROADSIDE/*page* 30

In this poem the sugar-canes, which are moved from cane-field to factory, are seen as representative of life and death of the majestic and the tawdry. The first two stanzas vividly contrast the past glory and present plight of the canes, but the rest of the poem does not develop this theme; it is merely repeated and finally seems a little overdone.

2-3. *you tossed . . . roadside:* the sound that the canes made when the wind blew on them.

5. *treasury of lost sound:* the canes cannot make the sounds they did before and so they seem to the poet to be storing up sounds they are no longer capable of making.

13. *tyranny of shining teeth:* people will eat the sugar-cane. It seems a rather pompous way of saying this.

18. *yearly sacrifices to power:* the canes must be ground for making sugar. The poet sees this as a rather futile and sad end for them.

TROY/*page* 31

'Troy' operates through two symbols—that of Hector, who has been killed by Achilles, and the roots and branches of a tree. Hector had to be killed if he was to survive in people's

93

minds, just as the tree has to go through its own cycle of 'death' during the dry season if it is to come to life during the rainy season. At certain stages of the poem the two symbols merge with telling force:

> Why must he fall
> When still a green branch

The answer is in the penultimate stanza where Hector's death is seen as a prelude to the actions of all who came after. This is why he is said to know 'the trunk of man, the branches of heroes and gods'. He comes to stand for all human endeavour and was greater than he realized.

'Troy' is not a difficult poem but Wilson Harris is dealing with a complex theme and he employs his symbols for their maximum effect. For instance note the contrast between the bright flower and the dark branch in lines 18–19; the bright flower suggests both life and hope. Through Hector and Achilles, Wilson Harris relates mortality and immortality. The paradox is that Hector would have liked to be Achilles.

1. *Hector:* During the war between the Greeks and Trojans, Hector and Achilles fought. Achilles slew Hector and dragged his corpse behind his chariot to the Greek ships.

4. *controversial tree:* In this stanza the whole history of man is built round the tree image. History produces heroes who themselves bring about history, just as roots produce leaves which fall and go back into the earth.

6. *eternity to season:* a permanence emerges from the ephemeral.

8. *So he must die to be free:* Hector has to die if he is to become a hero of all time. He must experience the truth about himself in order to know the worthlessness of former values.

14–16. *The everchanging . . . broken compassion:* Everything must alter, die and so gain peace within itself.

17-18. The wind suggests that death is not the end: rebirth will come about.

19-22. The dry leaf can be destroyed but not the brown root. Achilles cannot really destroy Hector. Note the suggestion of their conflict in *wheels of war*.

26. *scales:* the bark of the tree. Also musical scales.

27. *petals of space return:* the tree blooms again.

37-39. *To be . . . climb:* To discover himself must he die? Is Hector's humanity dependent on his becoming a god?

41. *Hades:* the underworld.

45. *capricious lightning of victory:* at one stage Hector felt he was winning.

46. *Achilles rests beside the ancient sea:* Sometime during the Trojan war Achilles retired in anger to his tent and refused to fight.

47. *death waits in the guise of immortality:* Achilles was himself slain by Paris.

57. *breast of love:* Hector is like Christ and really greater than Achilles; he bears the burden of man.

58. *The struggle that live and shines:* the tree comes to mean the persistence of man in trying to overcome all obstacles.

60. *the labour of all:* from Hector's death present-day mortals can understand the meaning of existence.

62. *contradiction:* he does not want to die yet has to, if he is to be immortal and to enrich his own experience.

65-67. *his red flowers . . . imperfection:* though Hector dies his heroism remains and helps to inspire those who come after.

66. *illusion:* immortality is the illusion.

SONG FOR MY BROTHERS AND COUSINS/*page* 34
Use of two basic rhymes throughout the poem, the repetition of two lines with variations and the three- and four-line stanzas suggest that the poet is attempting a variation of a

villanelle. (See 'Villanelle of the Living Pan' by Walter Adolphe Roberts.) But he does not restrict himself to this and he has a five-line stanza as well as 'us' which does not rhyme with any other word. The lyrical theme is well suited to a villanelle for it is simple and direct—the celebration of human comradeship.

1. *O what . . . torn away:* what one has come to cherish cannot be disregarded.

4. *Lovers will hear . . . away:* human beings who are fond of each other will not allow anything to hinder this love.

9. *giving they are gay:* in sharing what they have they are happy.

AND THE POUIS SING/*page* 35

Herbert's poem should be compared with Carter's; both poets are concerned with expressing the injustices that have been committed against the peasant in the West Indies. Carter was concerned with the slave and the plantation worker, Herbert with the Caribs. For Herbert the Caribs represent a state of innocence, when man was at one with the whole natural world; appropriately, therefore, the poem opens with a nostalgic glance at the past. Then the image of the hawk diving on the dove shatters the illusion; contact with the western world had started. The Caribs were not to have their innocence much longer.

Images attempt to show the bond that existed between man and nature; the inversion that occurs in stanza two when the 'children of the sun' realize that the sun is 'hostile' is a way of stating the break-up of sensibility that comes with western contact. The hawk and dove imagery return towards the end to suggest a new hope; the past cannot be wiped out and the Carib past is the past of all West Indians; it ensures a future that is full of enormous possibilities.

In a way the poem leaves one with a certain lack of satisfaction. The tone at times verges too closely on an anthem and slogans very often take the place of poetry. But the poem is carefully worked-out; one hardly notices the rhyme and the contracted lines that halt the pace only to become accelerated in the expansive lines that follow.

3–4. *fires of a sullen but tolerant sun:* compare this with line 19 where 'hostile grew the sun and pitiless'.

13. *cacique:* a Carib chief.

19–27. The whole of this stanza describes the way that the Caribs became separated from their natural environment and how they were subjected to punishment—both from nature and man.

25. *necrotic:* dying.

29. *springs of laughter ran dry:* compare this line with lines 5–7.

36. *slave and cacique:* the poet is suggesting that there is a link in suffering between the African slave and the Carib chief.

38. *columbarium:* this is a symbol of new hope. It is an extension of lines 11 and 12 and lines 32 and 33. The dove that has been destroyed (or was apparently destroyed) represents the future.

RHAPSODY ON A HILL/*page* 37

Through nature self-awareness comes about. The poem begins with descriptive phrases that are typical of West Indian nature poems and then through the religious aside, the *personal* side to nature is introduced. Both religious and personal aspects are combined in the realization that it is the protagonist's youth which enables him to experience Christianity. Several references re-inforce the point—the protagonist is as 'young as heaven', the sea is young and is 'sucking at the river's nipple', the sun is like 'a child's eye' and so on. One is prepared for the final stanza—the moment of perfection when the whole world is possessed by him. The vivid image of the universe like a top clinches the idea of youth taking possession of the world.

2. *cut:* design.

5–6. *knuckled showers/Bruising the light:* the violence with which rain falls.

13. *God is a child:* all creation seems young.

18. *Ararats:* Mt Ararat was where the ark landed after the flood. It is used here as a symbol of hope.

19. *dove:* the dove that Noah sent and also the Holy Spirit. The poet is saying that surely he does not need to sin in order to be redeemed.

34. *Call God by his first name:* know God intimately.

SOURIRE/*page* 39

Departure is described here—one suspects that the poet is leaving the West Indies for England. Use is made of devices which help to emphasize the agony: in 'for the world only a wave', the play on 'wave' (water/bid goodbye) is most effective and in 'my God/who so taketh wings to fly dieth a little', the archaism and the paradox emphasize the predicament of someone who is forced to leave but is not very willing. As in the previous poem the nature images help to deepen the significance of the experience. But here they arise out of a close observation—the mountains 'queue up', his dead body is 'a dry geometry of bones' and the ship slowly going out is said to have 'a firmly shifting deck'.

8. *Book a wave for the world:* across the water he sees hands bidding him goodbye; he realizes that he is paying a

heavy price to see the world. Note the ironic flippancy of a travel agent's brochure.

12. *Whoso taketh . . . a little:* whoever wants to leave his homeland loses something.

14. *geometry of bones:* something whose only significance is in the way it is assembled.

25. *Not an arrow . . . of targets:* he is leaving a tame-world behind him, one which had little to fight with and so much to fight against.

32. *freemasonries of whales:* the whales keep together.

48–51. *My God . . . horizon:* he would prefer not to have to go.

DEDICATION FROM AFAR: A SONG FOR MARIAN/*page* 41

Lamming's poem is, on one level, a poem in praise of Marian Anderson, an American Negro singer, on another it describes the frustration of an alien living away from his home-land. In the poem, 'Marian' comes to mean the symbol of the past, about which he cannot be sure, but which he nevertheless wants to treasure. Because of this vacillating attitude the poem has two different voices—a pastoral lyricism and a harsh bitter note. But it remains a very personal poem—the evolution of a certain viewpoint is stated (an emotional one), and how finally the poet comes to the tremendous perversion present in the last line of the poem. This is done through a series of long expansive sentences that seem to terminate abruptly with the last line.

Although a poet in exile, Lamming makes use of images of his homeland to emphasize the separation and the feeling of loss—the fish, for instance 'hoisting their freedom' are a reference to the flying fish of his native Barbados, the islands 'at anchor in the west' (appropriately couched in sea-terms) refer to the West Indies. Because he is handling the theme of colour, it would have been easy to overstate his case and make some of the assertions jar. But this in fact never happens; the theme of colour briefly mentioned in the second stanza is dropped and appears with much more force in the reconsideration of lines 43–46.

1–4. The point of the comparison is that the memory of Marian is the means through which the aliens can become less hurt by their predicament.

6–10. A purely personal reflection which spoils the universality towards which the poem aspires.

12. *Where memory and imagination meet:* he wonders how much of what he remembers is true and how much he had invented.

15. *Feathered emissaries at carolling dawn:* simply birds singing at dawn. This expression seems as overdone as 'met and were one' (line 24) seems trite. Compare also 'celluloid display' (line 32) where he simply means 'cinema'.

36. *burgeoning:* spreading.

44. *Nor charted courses for the heart's refusal:* nor ever planned to hate anyone.

46. *urged to register with the outlaws:* forced to become an alien and to believe in hatred and violence.

49. *What clocks shall register our waiting:* is there any way of estimating out fears and anxieties?

SWANS/*page 43*

In 'Swans', Lamming attempts less than in the previous poem, although it is more than a simple descriptive piece. He contrasts the majesty of the river-swans with the vulgarity of humans. There are the same long lines that were observed in the previous poem but here they give an effect of breathlessness and awe. The technique is perhaps more apparent and should be compared with Walcott's in 'The Yellow Cemetery'—the use of assonance, word-play and alliteration; in one case (line 11) the repetition of 'leaping' has the effect of turning the rhythm back upon itself so that it seems to move forward with renewed force.

After the ecstatic tone of the first two stanzas, a satirical note creeps in with the arrivals of humans. They are described as a 'circus', dogs are mentioned before 'dutiful masters' which does double duty for 'small boats' as well. The world of nature laughs at the antics of humans and in the opening lines of the penultimate stanza, the evening has taken their place and seems to possess human attributes. The last stanza is the least successful. There are a number of phrases which suggest much but do not seem to operate in a satisfactory manner—'blank desertion', 'a contagion of madness'. In addition the last two lines fail because of their blatant appeal to sentimentality.

3–5. To the poet it seems that the swans are like the light, part of the summer and part of the sea.

9. *a ritual of preening:* instinctively the birds keep trimming their feathers with their beaks.

30. Compare quietude lying at anchor with islands lying at anchor (line 52 of the previous poem). Lamming suggests a quiescent state.

FUTILITY/*page* 45

Written in two parts which are complementary to one another, this poem contrasts the withering of flowers laid at the grave of the protagonist with the longevity of revealed love. The comparison seems trite and commonplace by modern standards and this accusation is in no way mitigated when it is realized that MacArthur Lawrence wrote in the 1920's.

Although the poem follows a conventional rhyme pattern, the contraction in the last line and the repetition of 'the flowers are dead' serve to indicate a certain consciousness of technique. This is even clearer when it takes on a newer and fuller meaning in the last stanza. But the marching rhythm seems unsuited to the sombre nature of the experience. Furthermore there is also a certain illogicality in a dead man complaining about the unsuitability of his wreath. Finally one cannot be sure that a great deal is achieved by the dis-organization of syntax: 'you had thought' seems out of place in line 2 as does the 'then' in line 6.

KAIETEUR/*page 45*

A series of laudatory phrases culminating in a rhetorical question is at basis the form of this poem. Visually the arrangement seems relevant with the long lines and the broad stanza pattern. The second stanza attempts to dwell more on response rather than on objective description, but the division probably marks a shift in emphasis; in the first stanza the view is from the base of the fall, in the second from higher up.

   Kaieteur: a waterfall in Guyana, 822 feet high.
 4. *maelstrom:* the water falling in such a volume creates a whirlpool.
    troublous: angry, stormy.
 7. If the sightseer did not kneel in awe, he would feel that he was doing something wrong.
10. *freaking the flow of desultory light:* the falling water makes the light glitter.
14. *And feel not . . . greatly anew:* the sightseer becomes conscious of God.

JAFFO THE CALYPSONIAN/*page 46*

Few poems are of this nature in the entire gamut of West Indian verse. It is at once comical and sad and should be compared with Sherlock's 'A Goodbye for Daley'. Here the poem is simply about a man who sung beautiful calypsoes, not for some select audience, but for his rum-shop companions. He sang about serious matters and about his slave-past but his audience could not understand. He truly becomes a tragic figure when he is too ill to sing; the joke about how he stole spoons from the hospital nurses is not really intended to amuse the reader. It confirms Jaffo as a figure of tragedy.

2. *ping-pong drums:* steel-band drums. The ping-pong carries the melody in the steel-band.

4. *the sorrow and the bawdy farce:* the unhappiness and the coarse humour of his own life.

5. *tents:* where the newest and best-known calypsoes are sung at Carnival time.

8. *unsponsored:* no one asked him to sing.

12. *easier in pain . . . memory of it:* when he sang it was not so difficult for him to endure his hard life, but he never forgot about it.

14. *released from pain into remembered pain:* his present distress was lightened but he remembered his slave-past.

19. *unsung calypsoes:* all the sadness he had wanted to laugh over but which he never really managed to do.
    rat-trap rum shop: the customers are caught by their love of liquor.

ASCENSION/*page* 48

' Ascension', like the next poem 'Jacob and the Angel', is concerned with life after death. It is in the form of a prayer with an invocation. The overall tone is brought about by the short pointed lines, the repetitive phrases and the rhythm which rises and falls. In the poem arid desert scenery of the lowlands is associated with everyday life and its lack of spiritual compensation, and green mountain scenery with immortality and the ultimate reward. The poet probably intends us to read these as words spoken by Christ before the Ascension.

JACOB AND THE ANGEL/*page* 49
Should someone, the poet begins by asking, seek to live on in spite of his failing physical powers? The next two stanzas do not directly answer the question—they merely refer to the unsatisfactory nature of life as the poet sees it. He concludes that true knowledge arises more from contact with Heaven than earth. Again the prayer-like tone is found; here it stresses the reflective nature of the thought, and the use of sibilants throughout contribute to the effect of grandeur and silence. The poem has its origin in the story of Jacob to whom God and angels appeared during a journey through Bethel.

8–9. *the outer edge/of prayer:* prayer is directed at God and must reach Heaven to be effective. Earth seems far away.

9. *unexorcized inexorcizable:* he has tried to forget the questions that worry him but they will not be driven away.

16. *a pillow of cold stone:* Jacob's head was resting on a stone as he saw his vision. The poet is suggesting that in spite of this he was nearer to Heaven than earth.

LETTERS TO MARGARET/*page* 49
This belongs to a series of eight letters. What is divine love? the poem asks. And various definitions are put forward—it has brought about life, it is associated with religious belief. Man's attempts to be super-human are ridiculous and it is divine love that keeps him in check. The poem has an obvious

form; from a definition of 'love', 'faith', 'wishing', 'fate' and 'pride', the poet comes to 'song' (by which he means a hymn to God); this takes him back to 'love' and so the poem has completed a full round.

4–6. *Faith . . . in love:* belief in God, which determines how one lives, has its basis in divine love.

9–12. *Wishing . . . finite will:* merely hoping is not the same as belief in God, for the former simply arises out of a particular situation and is a mortal attempt to desire what is known.

18–20. *our single pride . . . earth and sky:* the only quality of which one can be sure is pride which boldly asserts that man can dominate the universe.

27–28. *the pure . . . motion:* in song man creates the very essence of God.

29–30. *God . . . dark towers:* God is sorry for man who, out of pride, seeks to oppose the will of Heaven.

SWEET ARE THE NIGHTS OF MAY/*page 51*
A nostalgic piece which makes its effect through the use of rich colour descriptions of all that the nights and mornings of May mean for the poet. The maximum effect is achieved by the pile-up of epithets before the various nouns and from the haunting repetition of 'sweet'.

8–9. *unexplored desires . . . soul:* wishes which are nevertheless there.

12. *Flowery coverts:* places concealed by flowers.

16–17. *these to them/Pure joy and wonder were:* to the mists the distant valleys seemed full of wonder.

I SHALL WAIT FOR THE MOON TO RISE/*page 52*
In a way this is a love-poem, in another way a nature poem. The moon is personified in terms of a maid wearing a white

apron and the patterns which moonlight weave in the sky are said to be done by a painter. This is a very gentle poem; one is seduced by the rhythm and the experience of man and moon. The couplet after the two six-line stanzas is a little different in tone—a little more harsh—but the last line returns one to the tone of the beginning of the poem. One of the special qualities of the poem is the speculative nature: the poet seems to suggest that he can be certain of little. The rising moon is pushed further into the future than his action of sitting down. At the end one does not know what the protagonist has been doing, nor indeed what he eventually does. But some of the more technical devices of the poetry are clear—the city round him is described in natural terms and the moon in human terms. Out of the marriage of the two a new vision comes about.

6. *Chinese tea garden:* open-air tea-garden.
   divi-divi tree: a shady tree with very feathery, dry wide-spreading leaves found all over Jamaica.
8. This is of course a symbol of her purity.

LIGHT LOVE/*page 52*

Love should be a painful experience, the poet says, if it is to be lasting. In contrast to the previous poem this one is very logical and the second stanza (with its repetitive pattern) emphasizes the ephemerality of the love-experience. Evocative phrases serve to suggest meanings beyond the most immediate—like 'a soft footfall' and 'a soft voice of shaken laughter'. The fine point of the poem is the last seven lines where the imagery indicates what the poet regards as a more lasting love; in contrast to the smooth sibilants of the earlier part of the poem, the rhythm here is rugged and disjointed.

7. *spread twilight-nimbus:* one lives in a world of fancy that does not last very long.

What is the real meaning of death, the poet asks? Is it something of which one has to be afraid? Or does it bring peace? The poet suggests that peace in death is brought about by religion. Because the subject-matter is commonplace, and the thought not particularly original, this becomes a difficult poem to judge if one is simply not to label it 'trite'. But, although there is sentimentality in the poem, and even a tendency to slip into easy devices of language, the image of death waiting in an ante-room is certainly a powerful one.

5–10. These lines suggests that death is almost voluntary.

THE SWALLOW/*page 55*

It seems not entirely irrelevant that 'The Swallow' and 'Twilight' belong to the 1880's and because of this the slightly archaic romanticizing is understandable. There is a familiar desire to escape from the everyday world and to live solely in a world of nature; and the swallow is the symbol of this escape. One cannot honestly pretend that there is anything 'West Indian' about this poem; it belongs to a certain convention of English verse and within that convention it is a successful poem. However Leo is able at times to rise above the serious limitations of this kind of versifying. For instance, the jerky effect of the couplets is broken in the first stanza when one long sentence describes the freedom of the bird in flight. Equally the poet's vision, of regions where 'eternal silence forever reigns', (line 24) shows imaginative insight.

2. *opal light:* the different colours of the sunset.

11. *Till the great earth . . . spectre shore:* so far away that the earth seems a shadow.

An attempt is made here towards a more detached and impersonal observation; some of the images are quite startling and recur in later West Indian poetry. Leo's personification of nature seems quite original in the poem—the trees have 'wildly floating hair' and the wind composes a 'rhyme of grace'. One feels that Leo is describing his own Guyanese world. In contrast to the previous piece also there is a largeness about the poem that arises out of contact with a vast landscape—he is not concerned with the carefully preserved nature scenery of the English countryside. The poem displays a striking economy, centering itself on the description of twilight and morning and doing it in the language of music. What comes over most of all, however, is the vigour and vitality which he attributes to his natural world.

3. *umbrageous:* shady.

5. *misereres:* the music accompanying the 51st Psalm—'Have mercy upon me, O God!'

16. *rhyme of grace:* holy song, hymn.

BALLAD OF CANGA/*page* 57

Although a number of stories are related here about Canga, in reality the poem loosely strings together an assortment of popular superstitions. Basically the poem is humorous in intention since Roach seems more than a little sceptical of Canga's powers; consequently there is some intentional exaggeration. But the narrative line and the etiological ending are in keeping with a certain type of West African folk-tale. The chief success of the poem however lies in the modified use of dialect which often provides a type of shorthand, breaking off abruptly, but saying much more to

the West Indian reader. Part of the final effect of the poem
is achieved by the quick snappy humour which explodes at
the end of most stanzas. But the poem has a serious purpose
as well; it debunks the power of the European and the
omnipotence of God. At the end it is Canga that triumphs.

5. *Ashantee:* Ashanti, a Ghana people.
7. *obeah:* magic.
8. *What he curse don't bless:* if he sets out to use his magic
   powers against something, no one can oppose him.
20. *baccra:* white.
22. *maroon:* to be a runaway slave.
27. *Damballa:* in Mali the God of Creation, in the West
    Indies a snake god.
31. *mullet:* small river fish.
36. *socouyan:* 'old higue' in Guyana; a person who could
    change into a ball of fire; normally a woman, she was
    able to fly and was supposed to suck people's blood.
59. *tie his mouth:* dialect for 'would not reply'.

TO MY MOTHER/*page 59*

'To My Mother', although very serious, does not contrast
with the preceding poem, for in both of them it is the poetic
thought which has made for the success of the poem. Here
Roach has successfully exploited the possibilities of a private
world; even his central symbol, the mother kneading bread,
is one taken from private experience and given new point
and significance by its transmutation into art.

This is a very visual poem; action is always taking place
immediately before one. Furthermore there is an excellent
display of verbal economy and the last line seems to be derived
naturally from all that the poet has previously written about
here. The opening images which suggest death and decay are

particularly moving and the 'bone' (strength) of line 4 means 'body' in line 12, 'frame' in line 14, and simply 'bones' in lines 22 and 23. By altering the meaning, even though very slightly, and finally returning to the most basic meaning, the poet brings about an amazing degree of variety.

If the poem can be said to make its main point in any two lines then they must be where Roach speaks of praising

> life's revival through the eternal year.
> I see death broken at each seed's rebirth.

The mother is not really old, cannot really die, for she is one with the 'peasant stock' (a boast that seems to jar slightly). Finally it is the natural images that lift the poem out of personal sentimentality and give it form and full meaning.

15. *Come of your middle years:* he was born long after his mother was an adolescent.

19–23. The mother becomes a Christ figure; she has been a martyr to her son.

23. *Golgotha:* where Christ was crucified.

26. *death broken at each seed's rebirth:* whenever something new comes to life, this is a defeat of death.

32. *stone:* pebble, and also the base his mother would use for kneading.

VILLANELLE OF THE LIVING PAN/*page* 61

Adolphe Roberts says, in the language of classical mythology, that the world of nature is very much with us, that its beauties can be awakened by the poet. In form this poem belongs to a strict type of verse; Roberts has observed the rules—there are five stanzas of three lines each and a final quatrain; there are only two rhymes throughout. As an exercise in style it is therefore successful but there are some unsatisfactory elements. The use of poetic archaisms and the forced blending of Greek pagan belief and the ritual of the Roman Catholic church in the fourth stanza seems to spoil the poem. On the whole, however, its success lies in its lyrical ease.

1. *Pan:* a Greek rural deity, upper part man, lower part goat. According to Plutarch in the time of Tiberius, Thamus, a pilot on a ship bound for Italy, was told to spread the news abroad that 'great Pan was dead'.
   brake: thicket.
2. *Aegean:* Greek.
4. The way that the vine leaves fall on him suggest that he has been buried by snow.
5. *laurel:* The importance of the tree here is that poets were decorated with laurel.
7. *cicadas:* insects with large transparent wings. They make a shrill chirping noise.
11. *Unction of soul:* a sacrament of the Roman Catholic Church performed on those about to die.
16. *Attic:* ancient Greece.

SUN IS A SHAPELY FIRE/*page* 62
The sun is a powerful force which has entered the poet and given him power. The poem develops from a personal note in the first stanza, to the effect of the sun on the earth in the second, and then its effect in the sky, which is the subject of the last stanza. The last three lines link the three qualities of the sun. On another level Seymour is writing about the attributes of race.

2. *white springs:* clouds.
4. *light heaps beneath my skin:* I feel power within me.
6. *darkening:* because it is giving off its power.

8. *tier:* pile up.

7–10. The image here is good and suggests the humility with which the trees worship the sun.

12. *sheet light:* light reflected by clouds.

13. *equal-vertical:* a reference to the length and direction of the rays.

19. *gossamer:* flimsy.

33. *retinue of worlds:* the planets. Note how the image associated with marching and dancing is continued until line 40.

A BEAUTY TOO OF TWISTED TREES/*page* 64

A good example of the re-arrangement of themes in West Indian verse—landscape description and Christian sentiments fuse in this poem. The tree is the one on which Christ was crucified. One is prepared for a revelation from the first stanza, so that the paradoxical conclusion towards the end of the poem is no suprise:

> All the world for those who see
> Hangs its hope on a twisted tree.

One of the weak points of the poem is a tendency to slip into easy Biblical prose.

2. *harsh insistence . . . trunk:* the fierceness of the wind causes the branches to grow twisted.

11–12. A reference to the circumstances of the birth of John the Baptist and how he later began his ministry after coming out of the desert round Jordan.

17–19. Ezekiel was a priest and prophet. In a vision God led him to a valley of dry bones and brought the bones to life.

20. Moses was told by God to strike a rock. In this way the children of Israel obtained water when crossing the desert.

POCOMANIA/*page 65*

This poem takes its name from a Jamaican religious sect which is characterized by their supposed ability to evoke the spirit within their converts, to enable them to make prophecies and revelations. The second stanza intentionally has an incantatory rhythm to emphasize the ritualistic nature of the ceremony. The middle of the poem is philosophic: What, the poet asks, is the significance of all that he has described in the second stanza? There is Asia with its idea of Christ 'the shepherd and his flock', and Africa with its 'ancient gods'. Then after an injunction by someone involved in the ceremony (appropriately couched in dialect) the poem comes to a climax in lines that vigorously describe the way that the dead take control of the living. This gives it a final dramatic effect.

1. *Long Mountain:* a mountain near Kingston.
7. The people are clothed in white and the poet sees them against the dark background of the night.
18. *wisdom mock:* they disregard what people normally accept.
34. *Fall and cry me sister now:* a woman has fallen down and shouts in a frenzy.

TREES HIS TESTAMENT: A GOODBYE FOR DALEY/*page 67*

Sherlock charts a delicate middle-course between a theme that is at once sad and funny. The main concern of this poem is with the poverty of Daley—one feels that he never really had a chance. In a breezy, although solemn manner, (in the vocabulary of a Negro spiritual) the reader is told of Daley's death. Then follows an account of his life with 'Hard Up' and 'Hungry Belly' as constant companions. These lines demonstrate the poet's social concern. But can one really be convinced about the plumber-turned-painter in the next stanza? Sherlock states that the satisfaction that Daley could not find in life he found in painting. Now that Daley is dead, the poem concludes, the paintings remain, as the crucifixion of Christ outlasts all.

15–16. Daley never had enough money nor food.

35–36. Daley wanted to paint because he was in search of something greater than merely trying to satisfy his hunger for food.

39–41. The imagery here suggests both the refusal of the occupants of the houses to give him work and the anxieties of his own mind.

42. *trees:* There is a suggestion here of the crucifixion.

58. *Dust the feet that walked beside him:* Daley's feet have become dust—Daley is dead.

64. *skull shaped hill top:* Golgotha.

65. *When the eye of day is clean:* morning.

MELLOW OBOE/*page* 69

M. G. Smith's allegorical poem begins in the manner of many other West Indian poems with a description of the sea, related through metaphor. Then one realizes that the poet has a more ambitious intention and this is to show that the sea-foam symbolizes for him some grand experience in life, to do with the resolution of conflict; a resolution that does not come about placidly but through vigour and pain. This is what he means by his lines:

O beautiful
O beautiful
The cruelty.

The poet is attempting to find images from the sea which have a permanent significance for all men. He tells us that time, night, the stars have all surrendered themselves to the foam.

1. *mellow oboe:* a soft but penetrating tone.
12. *falls fragment into foam:* is broken up and surrenders itself to the foam.
15. *nebular:* cloudy.
    luminous: full of light.

THE VISION COMES AND GOES/*page* 70

For M. G. Smith nature is, in this poem and in the previous one, a means through which he comes to a better understanding with all that is elusive. In a special sense this is a religious poem, concerned with the inner quality of experience. Smith, however, always relates it back to the external world. The variety in tone from lush lyricism to cryptic incantation and finally at the end to invocation, shows a development in the psyche of the protagonist. Here, as in other poems, M. G. Smith has introduced the note of ritual into the commonplace nature-descriptions and the whole world is transformed quite startlingly into one of wonder. All nature is his domain, the poet says, and he celebrates its unbounded freedom and its aliveness; and finally, as in the previous poem, its reconciliation in faith.

The poetry of M. G. Smith marks an important development in our poetry. Nature is not allowed to lie fallow but undergoes a series of rotations; it emerges as representative of the inner life of man. There is a frequent tendency to spoil the high point of the poetry by prosaic sermonizing, by seeking to equate too closely mystical and everyday experiences. But above all this, there is the very conscious craftsman, who in his verse technique reminds one of Basil MacFarlane and who has successfully linked spiritual zest with physical exhuberance.

6. *Nor gives the sun . . . than snows:* nature whether in tropical or temperate latitudes represents one basic truth.

19–20. *Touch that is . . . chance:* understanding comes about because it has to or by accident.

POEM/*page* 73

As far as tone is concerned this poem seems pitched two or three levels above the normal level. It has swelling overtures and is perfectly balanced from a rhythmical standpoint, with the eulogy contained between the words 'To those' found at the beginning and end of the poem. The syntactical device of making the reader wait until the final line for the main verb, has the effect of exploring the full tonal properties of the last words.

Telemaque's poem shows how the theme of Africa is synthesized in West Indian literature. Not only for him is it to do with Egypt, the Congo and the Guinea forest but also with American Negro spirituals. In spite of the public nature of the utterance the poem succeeds because Telemaque is consciously using a number of devices. For instance the sentence-epithets that follow 'who' gather force and momentum as the poem proceeds until, in the latter part, the lines expand into a swelling rhythm.

4. *Sphinx:* a colossal stone statue found near the Egyptian pyramids.

6. *Look down upon the centuries like yesterday:* it was built such a long time ago.

8. *Congo:* a river in Central Africa.

10. *Niger:* a river in West Africa.

15–17. These lines refer to African slaves who were forced to leave their past behind. 'Urns of history' is not quite suitable here; it is more usual for West Africans to bury their dead.

19. *bloody pains of toil:* a reference to slave-labour in the plantations.

20. *hawser:* a large rope for mooring. The poet thinks of their pain in appropriate sea-imagery.

ROOTS/*page* 73

A nostalgic piece which attempts to re-discover the meaning and significance of a West Indian childhood. The various stanzas are devoted to expressing aspects of this experience and their appeal to the protagonist's senses. The sombre note is absent; instead here there is ecstasy and delight in the sensuous, the indulging of emotions for their own sake. The poet again makes use of relative clauses which are piled up on one another to give a grand cumulative effect.

Through imagery Telemaque succeeds in showing the closeness that exists between the young boy and his natural environment; river water in his blood, stones are milk and his voice sounds with mountain doves. Appropriately at the end of the poem this association with nature is seen in mystical and religious terms, although the last three lines seem to be a tailing-off rather than a conclusive ending.

2. *immortelle:* flowers with a papery texture which retain their colour after being dried.

9. *curved shores:* a reference to the shape of the island.

117

19. *young meaning:* he understood the meaning of youth by looking at the phases of the moon.
27. *cus-cus:* dry grass with a strong aroma used for making fans and so on.
31. *poui:* yellow flowering tree.
36–37. *chasmed pilgrimage . . . return:* as he looks down from the top of the palm tree he realizes that he cannot fall.

A CITY'S DEATH BY FIRE/*page* 75
A sonnet written after a devastating fire in 1948 in Castries, the capital of St. Lucia. Its maximum effect is produced by the use of words and phrases in unusual situations and by certain happy coinages. The poem describes the ravages of the fire and concludes hopefully that destruction is necessary for physical and spiritual re-birth.

1. *hot gospeller:* the fire which had come to chastise.
   churched sky: This probably refers to the tower of the Roman Catholic cathedral. Also the sky was like a church and could not be destroyed; it was a symbol of the unchanging. Note how religious ideas are subtly introduced by these words 'gospeller' and 'churched'.
2. *by tallow:* candle-light. The small flame of the candle and its useful attributes, are contrasted with the powerful fire and its terrible results.
4. *wax:* a reference both to the candle and to a substance used for sealing letters. The poet is suggesting that he wants his words to be lasting and his poem to have universal implications.
5. *rubbled:* buildings that have been destroyed.
6. *like a liar:* because the houses had collapsed.
11. *hills were a flock of faiths:* he could hope and believe in life again when he thought of the hills.

Briefly, Walcott celebrates in this poem, written in a style
from which he has moved away, the triumph of human love
which outlasts the body. The immediate occasion for the
poem is a cemetery by the sea, but the poet uses the dead as a
way of highlighting the predicament of the living. They are
not subject to the vacillations of the living, they are happier.
The first section concludes by stating the inevitability of
death. In the next section the poet is concerned with those
who died at sea and whom he feels are more courageous.
The religious element is now more apparent and the poet
suggests that God is the only hope for the luckless living.
The final section concludes by establishing what the poet
means by 'love'—the perfect love between humans which is
only possible through God. Note the use of alliteration
throughout which does not always succeed. 'The Yellow
Cemetery' probably refers to Choc Cemetery in Castries.

2. *wearing white stone:* the dead are said to be dressed in
   their tomb-stones.
4. *drowning:* the dead are 'drowned' in the earth.
6. *unkeening:* they are not unhappy.
8–9. *Could they speak . . . froth:* if the dead could speak they
   would be like the sun and the sea. Note the introduction
   of religious imagery in 'bibleling' and in lines 10–11
   'bread', 'wine' and 'nails'.
11. *day of nails:* the dead suffered when they were alive.
19–20. *It is a blessing . . . fathom:* the dead are very fortunate
   and avoid the unhappiness of the living.
24. *flapping boast of the crowing sun:* at the dawning of each
   day when we feel proud to be alive.
   linen graves: the clothes of the living are their tomb-stones.
   Compare the dead in 1.2 'wearing white stone'.
31. The landscape is not the desert of John the Baptist.

34–35. *Against the brittle wick . . . wins:* even though human beings desperately want to live on forever, they all die in time. Two images, not very successfully married, are found here. The 'wind in the clock' (Time) is said to blow 'against the brittle wick of wishes' (man's desire to stay alive). Also the 'wind in the clock' (from the idea of *winding* the clock) is said to win, i.e. Time outlasts our desire to stay alive forever.

39–40. *a man's speech . . . is over:* a man can be passionate but in spite of this he has to die.

42. A reference to regeneration; the bushes will grow from the dead man.

50. They died alone and were buried without ceremony.

51–53. *the nunnery . . . denial:* the white woman who had rejected her black admirer can no longer do this in death.

52. *pardoner:* forgiving.

67. *grave of hair:* the grass that grows round her like hair. Also her own hair has become her grave.

68. *democratic dead:* all are equal.

69. *brought to book:* have to give an account of how they used up their lives.

71–74. Compare a similar conclusion in Keane's 'Rhapsody on a Hill', lines 39–47.

74. *kingdom of haven:* purity.

75. *wind of generations:* the tree shedding its leaves is like the older generation giving way to the new.

80. God had appeared to Moses in a burning bush.

84. *signatures of a lost Heaven remain:* the rainbow

88. *land like a green book:* valley between two hills.

89. *The Author and the Author's purpose:* God's reasons for creating the universe.

91. *leaf crossing:* the leaf falls and crosses the swallow's body; Walcott compares this with the act of benediction.
95. *mountain music, pylon words:* both are monumental.
97. *telling star:* the star tells of faith.
99. *cliche of his soul:* people speak of a soul but do not understand what this means.
100–101. *grace to atone . . . ailed alive:* every man has to atone for what was done before he was born.
103. *wicks weaken:* people die slowly.
  halls of the heartsun: deep within one's being.

OVER HERE/*page* 80
Daniel Williams describes the way that people love nature as a palliative to frustrated wish and longing. The poem is above all a moving hopeful piece as the fifth stanza shows; the egg that breaks is a symbol of the new hopes of West Indians. Finally even the landscape alters; it is no longer the intoxicating sensuous one of the third and fourth stanzas but through it man comes closer to his spiritual self.
1–2. *Islands . . . chain:* a description of how the islands are scattered.
  3. *wish inconstant:* we have never wanted the same things for long.
  5. *narcotic:* producing sleep.
8–9. *lotus pleasure:* delight in indolence.
9–10. *temporary brazen . . . taught:* we have not wanted to become rich because we know it does not last long.
21. *our blood is green:* we are a peasant people.

Biographical Notes

RAYMOND BARROW

—born 1920 in Belize City, British Honduras. He was educated at St. John's College, Belize and at Catherine's College, Cambridge and is now a civil servant. His work has been published in anthologies and been broadcast on the B.B.C.

VERA BELL

—born in Jamaica and educated at Wolmer's Girls' School. She entered the civil service after leaving school and held various posts before she retired. She edited the *Welfare Reporter* and afterwards migrated to England. She is also known as a short-story writer.

GEORGE CAMPBELL

—born in Jamaica but at present he lives in New York. His *First Poems* (1940) is an important landmark in the development of West Indian poetry.

MARTIN CARTER

—born 1927 in Guyana and educated Queen's College, Georgetown. He was at one time a member of the P.P.P. government and was detained in 1953. During this time some of his most poignant poetry was written. He is now a U.N. representative for Guyana in New York. His *Poems of Resistance* was published in 1954.

FRANK COLLYMORE

—born 1893 in Barbados and educated at Combermere School where he taught between 1910 and 1958. He was awarded an O.B.E. on retirement. He founded the literary journal *Bim* and has edited it since its foundation. He published four volumes of poems and a book on the Barbadian dialect.

JOHN FIGUEROA

—born 1920 in Jamaica He was educated in Jamaica, America and England and lectured at London University. Since 1958 he is Professor of Education at the University of West Indies. He has travelled widely and has published two volumes of verse.

A. N. FORDE

—born 1923 in Barbados and educated Harrison College, Barbados and University of Southampton. He was a teacher in Tobago between 1944 and 1957, then became a civil servant. At present he is deputy general manager of the Caribbean Broadcasting Corporation. He has published in local magazines and is also the author of a booklet, *Canes by the Roadside*.

WILSON HARRIS

—born 1921 in Guyana and educated at Queen's College. He was a land-surveyor for several years and published poetry locally from 1945 onwards including his well-known *Eternity to Season* (1954). He is now a professional novelist living in England.

A. L. HENDRICKS

—born Kingston, Jamaica in 1922 and educated at Jamaica College and in England. In 1950 he entered broadcasting and is now a director for a well-known television company. He has published a volume of poems *On This Mountain* (1965) in England.

C. L. HERBERT

—born Trinidad where he lives and works. Although he has never published a volume of his own, his work has been anthologized and broadcast.

E. McG. KEANE

—born St. Vincent in 1927 and educated locally at St. Vincent Grammar School where he taught between 1947 and 1952. He went to England and gave up studying for an English degree to devote his time to mastering the trumpet. At present he lives in Cologne, West Germany, where he is a jazz soloist with a prominent band. Besides contributions to *Bim* and 'Caribbean Voices' he has published two volumes of poetry.

GEORGE LAMMING

—born Barbados 1927. Educated in West Indies, he taught and lived in Trinidad for some years. He went to England in 1950 and since then has been a professional novelist. He has claimed in *The Pleasures of Exile* (1960) that poetry was his first love.

WALTER MacARTHUR LAWRENCE

—born 1896 in Georgetown, Guyana. He was educated at St. Thomas Scots School and Queen's College. He started writing for a local newspaper in 1920. He published his *Meditations* in 1929 and has been called 'the poet of Guyana'.

IAN MCDONALD

—born St. Augustine, Trinidad in 1933 and educated at Queen's Royal College, Port-of-Spain and Cambridge where he read History. At present he works with a firm in Guyana. He has had work published in *Kyk* and *Bim*.

BASIL MCFARLANE

—born 1922 in Kingston, Jamaica and educated at Jamaica College and Calabar High School. Apart from periods as a civil servant and in the R.A.F. in Britain, he has always been a journalist. He published *Jacob and the Angel and Other Poems* in 1952. He lives in Kingston. He is the son of J. E. Clare McFarlane.

J. E. CLARE MCFARLANE

—born 1894 in Spanish Town, Jamaica and educated at Cornwall College. He was a civil servant and became Financial Secretary. He published four volumes of verse, edited two anthologies and wrote a prose work. He died in 1962.

ROGER MAIS

—born 1905 in Jamaica and educated at Calabar High School. He worked as civil servant, journalist and photographer as well as in many other fields. He wrote novels, plays and poetry and was also an accomplished painter. He left Jamaica in 1951 and lived in Europe until 1954. He died a year later in Jamaica.

UNA MARSON

—born Jamaica in 1905 and educated at Hampton School, Malvern. She left in 1932 for England where she became a secretary to the League of Coloured Peoples and afterwards a private secretary to Emperor Haile Selassie during his exile in Britain. She returned to Jamaica in 1936 and in addition to launching various papers and periodicals, she produced her plays. In 1938 she was in England once more and worked for the B.B.C. She returned to Jamaica in 1947 and apart from a visit to America she remained home as a publisher, journalist and social worker until her death in 1965. She published four books of poems, the first, *Tropic Reveries* in 1930, and wrote and produced three plays.

EGBERT MARTIN

—born 1859 in Guyana and died in 1887. His father was a tailor and he lived in Georgetown. Although crippled he managed to publish his *Poetical Works* in London in 1883.

ERIC ROACH

—born Tobago in 1915 and attended the grammar school there. He has been a teacher and a soldier and more recently a journalist. His verse has been published locally and broadcast on 'Caribbean Voices'.

W. ADOLPHE ROBERTS

—born 1886 in Kingston. He was educated privately and in 1902 began work as a reporter for the *Daily Gleaner*. In 1904 he went to America where he wrote for and edited numerous magazines. He did not begin writing novels until his late forties and it was in 1951 that he returned to Jamaica. He died in England in 1962 but, at his wish, his ashes were placed in Mandeville Churchyard in Jamaica.

ARTHUR J. SEYMOUR
—born 1914 in Guyana and educated Queen's College. He has pioneered interest in poetry in the West Indies and was founder of *Kyk*. He began publishing his verse in 1940. For many years he was a civil servant but left Guyana in 1962 for Puerto Rico where he worked for the Caribbean Organization until 1964. He is now employed as a Community and Public Relations Officer with a bauxite firm.

PHILIP M. SHERLOCK
—born Jamaica in 1902, the son of a Methodist minister. He was educated locally and read for a London degree. After teaching at school and university level, he became Vice-Chancellor of the University of the West Indies in 1963. He has published history books and folk-tales, as well as his poetry in various anthologies.

M. G. SMITH
—born in Kingston in 1921. He was educated at Jamaica College and University College, London. He taught at the University of the West Indies between 1952 and 1961 and is now Professor of Anthropology at the University of California, Los Angeles.

HAROLD M. TELEMAQUE

—born Trinidad and educated locally. He has had his poetry broadcast on the B.B.C. and has appeared in anthologies as well as individual publications. He is now a teacher.

DEREK WALCOTT

—born Castries, St. Lucia 1930 and educated St. Mary's College, St. Lucia and University of the West Indies. He has been a teacher and a journalist and his plays have been performed in London and New York. He has published three volumes of verse.

DANIEL WILLIAMS

—born New York in 1927 and educated at St. Vincent Grammar School and King's College, London where he read Law. He is now a practising barrister. His poetry has been broadcast on the B.B.C. and has been published locally.

Index of Titles and First Lines